This is the latest and most advanced edition by America's leading authority on job and career change. The previous editions have sold more than 500,000 copies, and have received universal praise in hundreds of media. A representative sampling of reviewer comments on previous editions is listed below:

"An indispensable aid for the job hunter." **Business Week**

"A breakthrough manual which gives individuals a complete source of professional knowledge and all the materials needed to execute an effective campaign." **Personnel Journal**

"The best handbook for finding a better job!" **Chicago Today**

"Honest-to-God this tells you how to get a better job and contains some of the best advice I've ever read!" **Training in Business & Industry**

"The master reference on job hunting...makes available for the 1st time, many methods and techniques that have been available only from professional job hunting counselors." **Rockford, Ill., Register-Star**

"Contains every conceivable idea for people seeking employment." **Society of Professional Management Consultants**

"Job hunting made easy. The professional secrets of job hunting...all of them are here." **Purchasing Week**

"The techniques are capable of catapulting almost any average person into a position offering much greater financial rewards!" **The National Public Accountant**

"Advanced! Highly recommended!" **Vocational Guidance Quarterly**

"Just the cold, hard facts on how to ensure your getting that job you want. All the secrets are detailed! It's amazingly readable and highly recommended." **Scripps Howard "Memphis Press-Scimitar"**

"A professional program for getting a better job in all fields. Includes incredibly effective letters and resumes. Excellent new book. A good investment!" **Nation's Business**

"Hundreds of new ideas for people!" **Houston Chronicle**

"Many excellent tips, reference materials, and inside information." **St. Paul Pioneer Press**

"America's best selling job hunting book contains hundreds of new ideas for people seeking professional, managerial, or executive employment. Included are the latest and most advanced job hunting concepts." **San Bernardino Sun**

The Professional Job Changing System

World's Fastest Way To Get a Better Job

By Robert Jameson Gerberg

PerformanceDynamics
America's Leading Outplacement Firm

10th edition. Publication date: September 1, 1981
Copyright   1970, 1972, 1974, 1975, 1976, 1977, 1978, 1979, 1980,
             1981
             by Performance Dynamics, Inc.

Published by Performance Dynamics, Inc., Publishing Division
400 Lanidex Plaza, Parsippany, New Jersey 07054. Telephone
201-887-8800
Other offices: Alabama, Arizona, California, Colorado, Connecti-
               cut, District of Columbia, Florida, Georgia, Illinois,
               Kansas, Kentucky, Louisiana, Massachusetts,
               Michigan, Missouri, New Mexico, New York, Ohio,
               Oklahoma, Oregon, Pennsylvania, Texas, Utah,
               Washington, Wisconsin

ISBN: 0-912940-22-0
Library of Congress Catalog Card Number 81-83081
Printed in the United States of America

CONTENTS

**The Professional Job Changing System —
World's Fastest Way to Get a Better Job**

CHAPTER 1

Foreword

**About job
changing
in general**

...Few subjects are more potentially vital to a person's livelihood. Nevertheless, most people seriously overestimate their knowledge of job changing, the job market, and their own skills in this area. Job hunting is a most competitive activity. It is serious business.

...As a general rule, superior job hunting skills will compensate for lesser qualifications. Those who arrive at the "right time," whose personalities "mix," and who "appear" the best qualified, are the ones who get the jobs.

**About getting
the right
interviews**

...An increasingly sophisticated art. However, if you can identify the right targets — the more good contacts you make...the more good opportunities you will have to explore.

...One key to your success will be your ability to find the openings. If you rely solely on the "published job market" - the locally advertised or listed jobs - you may be looking for a long time; only 18% of all professional, managerial and executive jobs are advertised or listed with agencies or search firms.

About job security

... The higher you go in management, the greater the chance you will be dismissed. Your only real security will rest with your marketability and your personal marketing skill.

About the ideal resume

... There is no such thing as the ideal resume. However, for most executives the bio-narrative resume (your biography in narrative form) is the most consistently effective form of presentation.

... In general, the more your background is projected as a series of potential benefits...substantiated by accomplishments, the easier your job search will become. Also...successful job changers never underestimate their achievements.

About letters

... The combination of a cover letter and a standard resume will rarely produce as many interviews as a well-written letter. In a letter you can tailor your presentation, discuss what you can do or arouse curiosity. Besides, resumes make it easier for readers to discover a reason for disqualifying you.

About your interviews

... The first 5 minutes of many interviews are usually as important as all other minutes combined. Also, never beg for a job - you won't get it. Remember that once you've got the interview, your image and personality will be more important than your previous work experience.

...A winning formula for most interviews. Here it is: smart dress, a sincere

nature, a quick smile, and an interesting and enthusiastic personality. Combine these qualities and a talent for providing articulate answers to the interview questions in this book, and you'll start off by being 1 in 100.

About salary negotiations

...Employers like bargains, but they also expect job seekers to be looking for more money, and they don't like to hire the overqualified. Many candidates say that they're worth 30% more. Even if they settle for 20%, it helps convince the employer that they're pretty good.

...Always negotiate based upon the results you can produce. If you negotiate from your present income you will end up disappointed. Who wants to pay $40,000 for something that's going for $25,000?

About superior materials and targeting

...An executive mailed 1,500 letters and resumes and didn't receive an interview. We rewrote the materials and mailed another 300. It resulted in requests for 22 interviews. Superior creative work and proper target selection are critical.

About competition

...Most attractive advertised positions receive hundreds of applicants. This is because the average American professional changes jobs every 4 years and soon it will be every 3 years. In Europe, the frequency is not quite as great, but the direction is the same.

About the importance of marketing skills

...Job changing success depends 70% on personal marketing skills and 30% on background and ability. While you can't change your past, you can change how you communicate it.

About the career value of a job change

...Almost always in excess of $100,000, and often over $200,000. This is because when you land a higher paying job, you will probably maintain the salary differential for the rest of your career.

CHAPTER 2

Introduction

This book contains the general guidelines of a job changing system which people can use to move up in their field, or out to another field. It can be adapted and used by anyone seeking a position in a *professional, managerial, or executive capacity, and at any level from $25,000 to $300,000.*

As a program, it has already been used effectively by tens of thousands of people. This includes graduating students, commercial artists, scientists, union leaders, social workers, engineers, airline pilots, salesmen and company presidents.

It can work regardless of anyone's age, sex, education, or current employment status. In fact, with our methods, I believe you can achieve any reasonable job-related goal, including more challenge, a new career, higher pay or more satisfaction.

The basic key to this system is that it will have you execute a skillful marketing plan, and do so in a way that enables you to avoid much of your competition.

Perhaps best of all, the recommendations don't require "genius" or "luck." However, the system can fail if you treat the subject haphazardly or if you don't have faith in yourself. To make this system work, *you have to be willing to change.* You also need to read and understand this material, and then put the information into action. Last of all you need to give your job search your total commitment and dedication.

The Organization of This Book

This book is organized along the following lines. First of all, I will take you through the primary approaches you can use to generate interviews. The techniques which are provided should help you compete most favorably.

I will then review approaches for maintaining secrecy, handling references and completing application forms. The next area covers recommendations for the interview situation. Here I cover psychological tests, interview strategy, salary negotiations and contracts.

After that I will show you how outstanding resumes and letters may be developed, and how you can compensate for any *"liabilities."* Sample resumes and letters, along with a unique questionnaire, are provided. This last item can serve as your personal data base and help you to recall key facts for use in preparing your materials.

The last chapter contains a general *plan of action* and integrates the material covered earlier. It will give you a step-by-step checklist for planning and executing your campaign.

Some basic *reference information* is also detailed. Chapter 9 lists major executive search firms. Chapter 23 contains some added notes for women returning to the job market. Chapter 24 provides a *financial planning guide* for the unemployed. Chapter 25 lists the reference sources related to subjects discussed in various parts of this book.

I suggest that the first thing you do is scan all of the material. Every job changing situation is an individual case, and all of this information won't be new to you. However, chances are it will be worth your while to review everything.

When you read the material, you will find that the advice is sometimes grouped into three financial categories. Different recommendations may be appropriate for people seeking less than $25,000, for those seeking $25,000 to $50,000, and for those individuals who are seeking above $50,000.

Why People Change Jobs

People seek to change jobs for an almost endless variety of reasons. Some seek better pay, freedom from personality conflicts, inadequate conditions or office politics. Still others change because of a lack of recognition, responsibility, or diminished growth opportunities. Others are forced to look for new jobs because they have been fired from their previous position. All of these reasons are identical to those which prompted people to change jobs 30 years ago. However, today the frequency and acceptability of job changing has accelerated dramatically.

There are many forces behind this trend. Improvements in education, communications and transportation have all been stimulants. The general inflation has also contributed to a higher percentage of people seeking a change for financial reasons. During the early 1980's, the average person who accepts new employment will change jobs again within four years. In this decade people will continue to place self-interest ahead of previous traditions of organizational loyalty.

While some people express concern over the rate of job changing, it does provide certain advantages to our society. The principal benefit is that it facilitates a sharing of knowledge and experience. It also results in the skills of our people being applied in areas where they can be most productive. The fact that people do change, along with the resultant sharing of experience, is basic to the development of new businesses, industries and even countries.

In the future, job changing will be a rather inevitable event in the lives of most people. Because of this, to insure greatest personal growth, you need to view your talent and knowledge as something to be marketed for maximum profit and career satisfaction.

This requires *knowledge* of how to change jobs and the *ability* to turn this knowledge into action. Once you have mastered this book, the ability to change jobs should be a clear option, a basic consideration which is available to you in all future career decisions.

Job Hunting Competition

The competition for jobs is unique in that you cannot see your competitors. Because of this, many job seekers act much less keen and approach job changing with a minimum of drive. They also tend to relate to their past instead of to their future.

Apparently, few people realize that jobs at all levels are won by those (1) who become candidates and (2) who appear to be best qualified — *rather than those who are, in fact, best qualified.*

This year ten million people in the U.S., with incomes in excess of $10,000, will prepare and circulate resumes. Furthermore, over the next twelve-month period, almost every employee will devote some thought to possible job or career changes. While the competition for jobs cannot be precisely measured, there can be little doubt about its magnitude or existence.

How Most People Job Hunt

Nevertheless, the fact remains that 98% of all job seekers do a very poor job of marketing themselves. For example, typically, the first thing most job seekers do is write a resume. It tells a little bit about what they have done and where they did it. It is generally what I call a "tombstone" resume, reading something like "Here lies John Doe, born this day, went to these schools, had these jobs."

The problem with these resumes is that they make people look like everyone else . . . and they don't tell anything about what individuals can do for an organization. *(People sometimes forget it, but the only reason that they get hired is for what they can do.)*

Now, once most job seekers get a resume together . . . they usually invest $100 and have it typeset and printed. And that's the full extent of the investment they make in themselves!

The folly of this is that if they were dealing with anything but their own career, they'd probably never take a million-dollar product and try to sell it with a $100 marketing investment.

The fact is that most people are million-dollar products themselves. They usually have $500,000 . . . $1,000,000 . . . or even $2,000,000 worth of career left to count *(their future earnings capacity during the balance of their career).*

Of course with their resume printed, most people make a lot of other mistakes. They usually scatter their materials as they answer blind ads, visit a few agencies, go to a search firm or two, and contact some close friends. Their approach tends to be haphazard . . . they chase after dead-end leads . . . and their job search takes a long, long time. The remarkable part is that after taking these frustrating and scattered actions . . . they think they've run a job campaign. The basic reason for this problem is twofold. First of all most people don't begin to comprehend the magnitude of their competition and how it impacts their chances. The second reason, and perhaps the most basic cause of the problem, has to do with our educational system. I don't care how bright you may be, or whether you have multiple degrees from Harvard, Oxford or Cambridge, I can almost guarantee you that they didn't teach you how to market yourself or master the job markets. It's just not covered.

From my perspective, if people don't get knowledge "in school" or from a firm such as ours, they will simply never learn it. And that, in a nutshell, is why 98% of the public never master job hunting.

The Importance of The "Unpublished Market"

Some years ago I undertook a major study to determine how people at all levels found their jobs. It also sheds some light on why in the 1980's, a smart job campaign is a necessity.

What I found out is . . . if job seekers contacted all of the nation's tens of thousands of employment agency counselors, and if they reached all of the executive search consultants, and if they read every single one of the Sunday and daily papers every day for one solid year . . . then they'd get exposure to only 18% of all the positions in the country.

This is true because the agencies, newspapers, and search firms constitute the smaller and most competitive part of the job market . . . generally called "the published market." (I estimate that this is about 18% of the entire market.)

Why is this the case? Well, advertising is very expensive. There are also many firms that don't want to pay employment agency or executive recruiting fees.

The basic fact is that most firms prefer to avoid paying major recruiting expenses. Their jobs tend to be filled from within . . . from personal contacts . or through people who approach the right person in their firms at the right time. Because they are never advertised, or listed with agencies or recruiters . . . all of these openings are commonly referred to as "the unpublished job market." (This segment accounts for about 82% of the entire market.) Just what does all of this mean? The answer is that if you want to gain exposure to most jobs . . . you must thoroughly penetrate both the published and unpublished job markets, and this is what the approach in this book is designed to achieve.

The Timing of Your Job Campaign

Individuals frequently write to me about their job hunting success probabilities in various economies. I know of many individuals who delayed job campaigns because they saw that unemployment was very high, and assumed that jobs would be scarce. On the surface this observation may seem to make sense. However, during recent years when unemployment has been high, the reverse seems to have been partially true.

In the late 1970's when the media was focusing on unemployment, there was a concurrent shortage of job candidates in many fields. In fact, many search firms and agencies had listings for positions, but were unable to find candidates.

Our national psyche is shaped very much by the media. Bad news about unemployment serves to convince people that there are few jobs available. However, let's take a closer look at unemployment and job availability.

Unemployment is a scary word. As it is used in the United States, it is also very political and very misunderstood. For example, what if you were told that the total employed, or wanting employment, was 100 million, and that unemployment was 10%. The first thing that you might assume is that 10 million people have lost their positions and that there must be a tremendous shortage of jobs.

Now, if this hypothetical example broke down anything like our real-life situation, you'd quickly discover that neither of the above assumptions was remotely valid. Why? Well, when you would examine the 10 million figure closely, you would discover something like the following:

* 1.5 million were primarily very young people looking for their first jobs.

* 2.5 million had not been working, maybe not even looking, but then decided to look and had yet to find what they wanted.

* 1.5 million were simply people who quit their jobs, some prior to a sabbatical; others prior to going into their own business.

This would leave 4.5 million, out of a total population of more than 220 million. Then, out of this 4.5 figure, you should eliminate those who were on temporary layoffs (e.g. one or two weeks), as well as those who habitually work six months, but who really want the next six months off!

Anyway, what you would then have left would be a more realistic picture of the actual number of people either "fired" or permanently laid off. Whatever that number turns out to be, it is a serious matter. However, the percentage would be nothing like the original 10%.

Well, what about available jobs? The market for professional, managerial and executive jobs depends mostly on turnover. Annual national turnover in corporations is estimated at 25%. Every year millions of professionals, managers and executives change positions, and in 90% of the cases, their employers look for replacements.

The market is bolstered by the fact that employers are always phasing out old jobs and considering new ones, as well as replacing executives who have retired. A third significant source for management jobs stems from business expansion, new businesses and new industries.

During a severe recession the available positions from this latter source are quick to dry up. However, the basic market for management jobs, the part sustained by turnover, should always provide a substantial market.

From a seasonal standpoint, the "published job market" is slower during the summer months and in late November and December. During January, many firms begin searching for additional employees who have just been authorized under new annual budgets. As a general guideline, I recommend that you launch a job campaign when you feel your need exists, without particular concern about the season or the state of the economy.

CHAPTER 3

Prior to Starting & Where to Direct Your Campaign

This system of job changing depends upon the execution of a well-planned campaign. However, before you begin your job search, you must do some spade work. By taking care of details now, you will avoid frustrations which plague many job seekers. The major things which require your initial attention are discussed below.

You Need the Right Attitude

At any moment in time, there are qualified individuals who are saying (and believing) that *"it is simply impossible to locate a decent job."* However, their attitude and lack of self-confidence may be their only job-seeking barrier.

If you are seriously thinking about a better position, then you must place your campaign at the top of all personal priorities. In order to take maximum advantage of this system, your job search should be approached with the same spirit that you would apply to anything else you really wanted to accomplish.

If you are someone who has been job hunting for some time, you probably need to start by recognizing that your present approach is inadequate. Then you should use this system as a base for launching an entirely new campaign.

This may require a great effort to dismiss the discouragement associated with your past efforts. *(I say this because there is nothing more ego-shattering than the experience of job hunting without success.)* Nevertheless, if this is your situation, it will be essential for you to work steadily at a new campaign, and do it within the right mental framework.

You Need Job Hunting Goals

I am always surprised at the number of people who have difficulty in deciding upon what they want, and who subsequently postpone job campaigns. However, in order to conduct an effective campaign, you must first arrive at specific job, title and financial objectives. Quite frequently, people must compel themselves to select some such goals in order to get their campaign moving. This is not unusual, and many people begin a search and then refine objectives later.

If you are unhappy where you are, and uncertain as to what job to seek, you might consider the following. Begin by making a list of all the things you really "want" out of a job. These may include factors such as:

new friends	people contact
different career field	desk work
security	creative work
prestige and title	independence
authority over people	more challenge
authority over budgets	shorter commute
higher salary	more time for family
ownership or part equity	chance for growth
travel	more excitement
physical work	lack of pressure
mental work	better hours/part time
geographic location	comfortable office

These are just some examples. However, after you've prepared a listing, you should organize it by priority. The next step would be to identify specific industries and jobs that will offer you the best chance for achieving your objectives. Obviously, these need to be reconciled with the marketability of your skills, and experience . . . but don't rule out career change or high financial goals.

If you get stalled on this exercise, you may need some professional advice on your marketability and career options. However, before doing that I think that listing your strengths, weaknesses and preliminary objectives may be a helpful way to focus your thinking. Writing things down also makes it easier to achieve personal discipline, as written words often have a way of becoming "unbreakable" goals. It may force you to make some necessary decisions.

You Need Information About Yourself

You will need to assemble everything about yourself that might be of potential marketing value. In the back of this book, I have included a questionnaire which will help you organize this information. Or, you may choose to assemble it by making notes and gathering old resumes and job search letters.

The form of this information is not important. But collecting it *now* is very key. If you were a salesman selling a product, your starting point would be to learn the features of what you have to sell. As a job hunter, you are both the salesman and the product. This information will serve as the basis for any resumes or letters you try to develop. You should collect it all before you begin thinking about "how" you are going to communicate your assets to others.

You Need an Outstanding Resume

From your data base, you probably will have to develop one or two resumes which are superior expressions of your talents and background. In the resume section you will find guidance for doing this with a minimum of inconvenience.

Most people will use their resume to help create their own breaks, and to get interviews with the right people at the right time. It must be clean, distinctive and easy to read. At the executive level, it must also be a persuasive soft-sell advertisement which is prepared in excellent taste. For most people, the most effective resumes are ones that sell ability and talent rather than just experience. Creativity, in good taste, is a prerequisite for those who seek something more than modest salary increases.

You Need Outstanding Letters

You will also need to prepare your resume in letter form, as you will encounter many situations that call for a letter rather than a resume. This is particularly true for people seeking positions in Europe. In addition, certain firms (and advertisements) will request that you write about yourself rather than send a printed summary.

Letters will be especially important if you are seeking a position above $40,000 or are considering either a variety of positions or a change in careers. Different materials will be required for contacting executive search firms, corporations, or answering advertisements, as well as for mailing to people in different industries. Again, for your guidance, samples are included in a later section of this book.

As important as resumes and letters are, the fact that you have some outstanding materials will be no guarantee of success. The determining factor will be how well you use them.

Where to Direct Your Campaign

Any job campaign must have direction in terms of the key industries and companies of interest. You should start by preparing a list of all firms that are prime candidates for your talents. Obviously, you are going to find other opportunities, but these should normally get the attention of your first efforts.

Ordinarily you should consider approaching the companies in your industry and the firms serving it both *vertically and horizontally.* These are the people who would value your experience the most. Another primary target group would be *allied* industries. For example, if you are working for a camera manufacturer, you should try to reach firms that sell other consumer durable products.

Firms in the same general field often market in similar ways, organize along similar lines, and face similar problems. In some cases, dependent upon your specialty, your initial effort should be directed at firms which are the *same size* as your present employer. For example, if you were in accounting, you might want to seek employment with firms which are likely to utilize similar systems and procedures.

Unless you want to relocate, you should also restrict your initial efforts to companies in your immediate geographical area. In most cases, these will be the firms you can visit without taking excessive personal time for interviews.

Try not to spend time in seeking positions with school-oriented banks, brokerage and law firms. If you are looking to get ahead, there are still many firms where your lack of attendance at the "right" school(s) will put you at a marked disadvantage. You should be able to identify these firms in the course of normal social and business conversations. *(If you do have the right school background, you should, of course, take maximum advantage of it.)*

Large vs. Small . . . Strong vs. Weak Firms

There is always a question as to whether people should direct their campaign toward large or small companies, or financially strong or weak firms.

The choice between large and small companies is generally a matter of personal preference and individual background. For young people starting their careers, the large firms can usually offer higher initial pay and more formalized training. Once you've been working a few years, small firms may have more appeal. They are more likely to have a distinct personality and a feeling of team spirit. Often they can also offer more independence and room for achievement.

As far as financial strength is concerned, it has been my experience that firms in trouble should never be eliminated from consideration. At a top-management level they can be of particular interest. In approaching such firms your competition will generally be less, and their problems may be your opportunity for achievement. Companies with problems can also be more flexible in salaries and contract negotiations.

You can identify the types of firms mentioned above by reading the financial magazines and business papers. With such firms I generally recommend that you contact a very senior executive on a direct personal letter basis. Before writing them, you should certainly research the firms, and subsequently orient your written communications to their immediate problem areas.

Rapidly Expanding Corporations

You may also wish to contact expanding firms within growth industries. These are the companies which will have to seek junior and senior talent from the outside, even if they generally try to promote from within.

One source for names of these firms is *Financial World* magazine (New York, N.Y.). They publish a special annual directory issue on the fastest growing firms.

I also suggest you check the Business Periodical Index under "Growth Firms." Many business magazines have quarterly listings of the firms enjoying above-average growth. This index will provide you with the magazine and issue in which the information appeared. This may be particularly important if job openings are scarce in your own industry.

Developing Interviews

In the following sections some major channels for developing interviews are reviewed. In each case you will find techniques which can set you apart from most other job seekers who are using the same avenues. These include:

* *Personal Contacts*
* *Answering Advertisements*
* *Placing Advertisements*
* *Direct Mail to Employers*
* *Employment Agencies*
* *Executive Search Firms*
* *Professional Associations*

In some situations an individual will not have to use all of these channels. Nevertheless, you should review each channel in light of your own situation and goals. A campaign which uses many of them will usually be in order.

CHAPTER 4

The Development and Use of Personal Contacts

Personal recommendations are responsible for millions of people securing employment each year. In fact, the most popular way to seek interviews is through personal contacts. As a general rule, the higher you are, the more important they become.

These contacts may include former employers, suppliers, business associates, priests, rabbis, ministers, alumni from your college or fraternity, social and community contacts, insurance agents, bankers, merchants, friends, relatives, former teachers, trade association officers, attorneys, congressmen, senators, etc. *(When you're unemployed, your creditors may be the best contacts of all!)*

If you are seeking a position above $50,000, you may have to rely more heavily on developing leads through contacts. At the same time, you should be alert to a very common mistake. Many people end up wasting a lot of time that could have been better spent elsewhere.

People often think that their wealth of contacts will make job hunting easy. However, this rarely turns out to be the case. Remember that personal associates will have a tendency to provide you with interviews as a courtesy. Also, people often exaggerate their potential knowledge of suitable openings and their general ability to help.

I think that before you use your personal contacts, it is wise to let your campaign get underway by exploring other approaches. For employed individuals, the best policy in the initial stage is to keep your job hunting plans to yourself. I am frequently amazed by the sophisticated people who fail to do this, and who quickly create personal difficulties for themselves. Of even more significance, they rapidly dilute the potential effectiveness of their really good contacts.

After you have launched your campaign, you may also refine your position and financial goals. This is another reason for waiting until that stage before you try to use your contacts. Then, when you do approach them, your object should be to see if within their circle of acquaintances, there were any persons who might be interested in the benefits you could bring their organization.

Developing Contacts Through Advice Letters

In terms of developing personal contacts from a zero level, there are techniques which I have seen prove successful on many occasions. For example, if you are a junior level or seeking your first civilian job, I suggest that you encourage suggestions from senior executives concerning the direction of your career.

You could even consider seeking advice by writing top executives with whom you are not personally acquainted. Of course, your "advice letter" would have to be well phrased. You must convey your respect for their authority and expertise on these matters in an appealing way. The object is to have this result in their taking more than a passing interest in your success. During any discussions you should also lay the groundwork for additional phone call contact during the course of your job search. Your objective would be to obtain job opening leads in either the firms of these executives or their associates.

In the last paragraph, I was referring to a strategy for people under $25,000. Any senior person using an "advice letter" is likely to be pegged right away. If you want to explore this method, your letter should include a disclaimer about "looking for a job." Is this your type of style? Let me give you an example of this letter.

Dear Mr. _____:

I am in need of some personal advice. And, since I think you are one of the few people who is qualified to help me, I thought I would ask for a favor. Even though we are not acquaintances, I am hoping you can give me a moment.

For some time, I have been grappling with a critical career decision. You see, by mutual agreement, Rockford and I have decided to part. I am leaving on amicable terms, and because of some significant contributions, the company is fully supporting me in my job search.

I am a strong results-oriented professional executive, with across-the-board P&L experience in many businesses. What I am trying to do is to "focus" on those most critical aspects of my experience, and your intuitive reaction would be invaluable to me.

Now I realize that given my statement, this may appear to be an employment application. However, I assure you that this is not the intent of this letter. I would not waste your personal time by pursuing the vanishingly small probability that your firm needs me at this particular time. My resume is attached for only one purpose. It is to give you a summary of my experience on the chance that you will respond to my sincerity in seeking advice from you.

I will take the liberty of calling your secretary in a few days to see if you have been able to fit me into your schedule. My thanks in advance, and I will be looking forward to seeing you.

Very truly yours,

Shrewd? Perhaps. This approach would produce some interviews. Whether it's worthwhile is another question.

Some time ago I was visited by a gentleman who had been told by a career counseling firm in Philadelphia to use this type of campaign. He was getting in to see some executives. However, it took him forever, and he felt uneasy about using a method that was less than ethical. He also had been through some embarrassing moments with people who saw through this ploy, and who told him what they thought. Anyway, my advice is to first try the straightforward approaches covered in succeeding chapters.

Developing Contacts Through Pyramiding

Another strategy for expanding contacts is called "pyramiding." This involves capitalizing on the name of one individual to gain an interview with another. Your purpose would be to use the power of one name to gain an interview in a secondary firm.

For example, if you were meeting with the executive of a company and you felt that the interview would not produce anything, you could lead into a discussion concerning another firm. You would then ask your interviewer whether or not he felt that it would be a firm for you to explore. At the very least, he is likely to routinely say:

> *"Of course, you ought to contact them."*

Your next step would be to write the president of the new firm, something like the following:

> *"In my recent meeting with Mr. X, he suggested that it might be of value if I arranged to speak with you."*

If handled properly, this strategy of pyramiding can be enormously effective. We have seen individuals conduct entire job campaigns using this simple technique for getting interviews. In terms of the level of application, it will prove most effective for those in junior or middle management. If you are seeking a top-level position, the process becomes more delicate since verbal contact may take place between one company executive and another.

Remember, in high-level situations, personal recommendations count more than anything else, and any thoughts about pyramiding should be carefully evaluated. The major negative of this technique is that the process of developing personal contacts is time consuming. In order to make your efforts effective, you will have to be a careful planner and a good record keeper.

Developing Contacts From a Zero Base

In the previous section, I talked about building personal contacts by "pyramiding," or asking existing contacts for the names of other people who might be helpful to you. If you have very few personal contacts to start with, however, it is still possible to rapidly develop a large number of contacts. Some of the more effective methods are described on the following pages.

Contacting Prominent Influentials

Many of my clients have generated interviews by writing to prominent people. In one instance, a young woman from Boston wanted to relocate to Minneapolis. Unfortunately, she had no connections there. I helped her launch a highly targeted direct mail and telephone campaign, and within ten days she was able to develop six interviews from referrals provided by Board members of three banks.

Governors, Senators, State Senators and politicians at almost any level can also be an excellent source for referrals. The same holds true for prominent doctors and lawyers who speak with many people during the course of each day.

Clergymen, accountants, hospital trustees, members of the Chamber of Commerce or other civic groups, members or employees of industrial development boards, investment bankers, insurance brokers and many others also fall into this category.

Contacting Everyday "Influentials"

A word of caution. Please don't fall into the trap of thinking that influentials are only people with power or prominence. Instead, think of an influential as anyone who might have some influence on your obtaining a job offer.

While people in highly visible roles can be influential for almost anyone, there are many people who would not generally be considered influential, but who can be helpful to you.

For example, if you were an engineer and were interested in joining a particular firm, you could call that firm and ask to be connected to one of the departments such as electrical or mechanical engineering. You could then explain your situation to the person who answers, and ask for a referral to someone who would be kind enough to take a few minutes to speak with you.

Chances are, this way you will be able to make at least one friend in the organization. Whether you start with another engineer, a salesman or a secretary, you can find an ally within the organization who can keep you informed of developments and introduce you to others at the right time. Most people are eager to help others who need assistance in finding a new job, and you will find that it is surprisingly easy to develop a network of contacts with people you have not previously known.

Your "influential" does not even have to be an employee of a target company. In one case I remember, a client developed several contacts by becoming friendly with the manager of a local New York area airport. The presidents of many local firms kept their company planes there, and the manager knew them quite well. He offered to provide introductions to a dozen of them. However, as it turned out, only three were necessary before our client obtained an ideal offer.

Developing Contacts Through Part-time Occupations

Today, it is common for many people to have a second job on a part-time basis. One of my clients, an ambitious MBA in his late 20's, took a job as a limousine driver three evenings each week. His assignments involved meeting executives at Newark International Airport and driving them to their homes in northern New Jersey and Westchester County.

By the eighth week of his part-time job he had a list of 13 executives he could call, and in the next four weeks he succeeded in generating three job offers through these top-level contacts. They included positions with Mercedes, Seagram's and Warner-Lambert's Consumer Product Division.

Developing Contacts Through Social/Civic Activities

Anyone who is considering a job search should make a real effort to meet and cultivate people who may be of assistance. However, the best time to do this is before you need to aggressively begin a job campaign. Aside from keeping in touch with your existing associates, you can generally expand your potential leads by making an effort toward active participation in the social side of business. I mean doing everything from dining in restaurants patronized by those in your field, through attending seminars, parties, trade association and supplier meetings.

If you've never been an extrovert, the time to start is when you know you are going to need a new job. Also, at all times you should keep some record of the names of individuals you meet. One of the best ways to *impress* is to be able to quickly recall someone's name from a single brief meeting.

If you can achieve even a small degree of prominence, this could bring you leads and make it much easier to develop and expand existing contacts. If you have any writing talent, you might try your hand at authoring some articles and submit them to the trade press.

Anything you can do to gain increased visibility will result in easier initiation of new contacts. Taking an active role in community affairs, politics and service clubs, along with speaking at seminars and trade associations, will serve as a means of accomplishing the same end. Let me give you an example of just how this can work. A woman in her mid-40's was relocated from Philadelphia to Lake Forest, Illinois. This had been necessitated because of her husband's promotion.

After arriving at Lake Forest, it took her a number of weeks to get settled in her new house, and then she volunteered to work actively in the campaign of a candidate running for Town Council. In the course of the next six weeks she met a number of people who offered to introduce her to people they knew. She made effective use of these introductions and shortly after the local political campaign ended, this woman took a newly created position as an Administrative Manager at the Headquarters of

McDonald's Corporation, just outside of Chicago. The position offered her far more challenge and responsibility than she had previously enjoyed.

Developing Contacts Through Major Events

Trade shows and conventions can be a very efficient medium for developing contacts. In one location you usually have dozens of people assembled, all of whom are associated with an industry of interest to you, and all of whom are there because they want to talk to people.

In these situations, people at all levels are usually present. If you are not able to make a contact at the management level, you can at least make a friend down the line. This person can then serve as your starting point for making higher contacts within the company.

For example, a sales assistant can introduce you to a salesman, who can introduce you to a branch manager, who can introduce you to a regional manager, who can introduce you to a general manager of a division. Of course, the higher you can start the better, but the important thing is to at least start someplace.

If you are unable to gain admittance to a convention or trade show, there are other options. For example, it is relatively easy to identify all the companies attending. They are often printed in a brochure available in advance of the show, and sometimes they are listed on an information board.

One imaginative client of mine, a Branch Sales Manager, went to a convention and visited each of the major hotels where the conventioneers were staying. Through a determined personal effort, he met dozens of people in both hotel lobbies and hospitality suites hosted by organizations. As it turned out, the informal atmosphere paved the way for his development of contacts with those who could help him. Within days he had lined up all the employment interviews he needed, and within four weeks he began a new position with Coca Cola Bottling Company of New York.

The Spot Opportunity Approach

Many of my clients have won job offers by cleverly anticipating an organization's needs. They did this by screening information which came their way, and identifying anything which contained the seeds of an employment opportunity.

Their vehicle for accomplishing this included reading the trade press for every industry and occupation interest, as well as general business magazines and local newspapers and magazines.

In their daily reading, they made notes of such events as expansions, new products, reorganizations, plant openings and promotions. Sometimes a feature article would highlight an expanding and progressive company. In some instances, advertisements supplied the tip that an opportunity might be in the making.

Over the years, I have learned that bad news can also be a source of employment opportunity. Bankruptcies, articles featuring the problems of companies (or industries) and their competitive struggles, are usually indications that the firms would welcome talent which could help them.

These opportunities can also be identified through other sources. For example, news about products and expansion plans often comes up at trade shows before being mentioned in the press. Construction bids and financings can serve as another type of early warning system as well.

The point I would like you to remember here is simple. Don't turn off your radar when you stop reading. As you go through your job search, constantly question everything you see and hear in terms of "is there an opportunity here for me?" I think you'll be surprised at the number of opportunities which have been passing you by each day.

As soon as you spot an opportunity, look up the address and phone number of the organization in question. There are numerous directories which can help you, and many sources are listed later in this book. If the company's name is not mentioned, there are even directories which cross-reference the names of individual executives with various organizations.

Your next step is to write the appropriate person, stating that you noticed the event, and that it would seem to indicate a need for someone with your talents. If you do not receive an answer, be sure to follow up with a phone call or second letter.

There are many advantages to this approach. The main point is that your letter will generally reach the person at a time when they are quite likely to need help. Your letter will also be a favorable reflection on your foresight and interest in the organization. Best of all, it is likely that you will have little or no competition.

Using this approach, a client of mine, an electrical engineer, read about a contracting firm in the northwest which was growing despite a broad industry decline. Their operational method included hiring people with specialized talents and then bidding on sophisticated projects all over the country.

The client wrote the President of the organization who had been mentioned in the article. He told him what an inspiration it was to read about an aggressive firm which didn't let an industry-wide recession interfere with its own plans for growth. He also mentioned his own electrical engineering specialty, and indicated how much he would like to be part of the type of organization the President had fashioned.

In response, he received an application form which was immediately submitted. However, he heard nothing further.

After two weeks, he wrote a second letter restating his interest in the firm. Then, after waiting another two weeks he wrote a third time of his desire to join the company.

His reply to his third contact was an airline ticket with a note from the President, "Anyone who wants to be a part of my firm that much, I would like to talk to myself. Get up here as quickly as possible."

This client went on to win other offers, but the one he ultimately accepted was an offer he received the very next day from the President of that same organization.

People who have used what I refer to as the spot opportunity method, have been able to uncover as many as 10 meaningful opportunities each day. You will find that this is not only an effective method for uncovering potential employers, but can also prove to be very informative and enjoyable.

Concluding Comments on the Use of Contacts

There are literally hundreds of things that enterprising people have done to expand their useful contacts. The few examples cited here should serve to stimulate your thinking about the things you can do, and the kinds of people who can help you to expand your network of friends and acquaintances.

Throughout your campaign, one of your best sources for information and personal leads can be from other people who are seeking new jobs. This may reach you through friends or on a direct basis.

For example, if you are in an executive position, you would be able to get a surprising number of useful leads from discussions with individuals whose resumes cross your desk. Remember, from a competitive standpoint, you owe it to yourself to learn about every routine source for identifying executive openings of potential interest.

You will also find it useful to check with any friends who have recently accepted new positions. If they happen to be in the same field, they may be able to supply you with a number of leads on positions which still remain open.

In the course of our consulting, the knowledge we have gained about the management of contacts would require a separate book to communicate. Nevertheless, if you implement along the lines of the highlights presented in these few pages, your job search should benefit immensely.

CHAPTER 5

Answering Advertisements

When people begin to look for a new job, their starting place is usually their local newspaper. Every Sunday, and to a lesser extent on some weekdays, millions of people scan the help-wanted pages. Unfortunately, not all job openings are advertised in local newspapers. Some employers never advertise their openings, while others make use of regional and national media.

As you might expect, there are many consistent advertisers in the help-wanted pages. They generally fall within three categories and include *larger corporations, executive recruiters and employment agencies.*

The advertisements by the agencies tend to create an illusion of more job openings than really exist. This is because a single opening is often listed by many agencies and advertised week after week until the position is filled.

The fact that millions of people concentrate on their local help-wanted ads is precisely why you should avoid too much reliance on this source. My years of experience in seeing people look for jobs have led me to form very definite ideas about the way people should handle job advertisements. However, even with the best techniques for answering ads, it will be very difficult for you to secure enough interviews through your local newspaper to generate a *number of offers.*

For one thing, as mentioned, many openings are never locally advertised. Secondly, your qualifications will be forced to directly compete with hundreds of job seekers. *(A display advertisement for a management job in The New York Sunday Times Business Section can generate anywhere from a low of 30 replies to a high of about 1,000.)*

In spite of the competition just cited, with superior materials and the procedures set forth on the following pages, you will be able to develop employment possibilities through answering ads.

The emphasis which you place on the help-wanted pages should normally vary in inverse proportion to the salary you seek. If you are looking for $25,000, you should be able to do quite well. If you are seeking $50,000, you won't find many ads and it will be much more difficult. The higher the salary, the lower the probability that a job will be filled through an advertisement. *(To gain access to any quantity of higher executive positions, you must read the regional and national media that are regularly used for recruiting senior talent.)*

Where to Locate Position Ads

Since your response to ads may bring only a small percentage of interviews, you are going to have to answer a great many of them. If you are seeking more than an entry level professional or management job, I suggest you do more than simply follow the ads in your local Sunday paper.

There are a number of key media in the U.S. in which employers regularly advertise for positions throughout the country. These include the Sunday editions of *The New York Times, The Los Angeles Times,* and *The Chicago Tribune,* as well as all four regional editions of *The Wall Street Journal.*

You should also check your industry trade magazines as well as publications which specialize in your occupational field. The Sunday papers I have mentioned carry advertisements for jobs in both their classified sections and business sections, as well as in their education and health sections.

Most advertisers do restrict their initial ads to the geographic area where an opportunity exists. However, I know of numerous instances where people have landed good jobs on the West Coast through advertisements in the Eastern newspapers.

At the end of the next chapter I have included a listing of the major newspapers which carry extensive help-wanted advertising.

In addition, a publication entitled *The Standard Periodical Directory* will provide you with the addresses of all newspapers or magazines in which you might have a short-term interest.

Selecting the Ads to Answer

Employers rarely find people who meet all the criteria they specify in an advertisement. Accordingly, you should never restrict your replies to those ads which sound exactly suited to your talents. *Answer ads even where there is a request for industry experience (or degrees) which you do not possess.*

When you respond to what seems to be a more senior position, your appeal may be because of your availability at a lower salary. Also, on advertisements for executive positions, you will often find that the individual eventually hired will be looking for new subordinates, and information on interesting people is occasionally kept on hand.

If you are just starting your campaign, I suggest that you go back and answer all appropriate advertisements that have appeared during the past 10 weeks. Most good positions take months to fill (even though they are only advertised once or twice).

In addition, if you develop some new resumes and letters after reading this book, you should send a new reply to the attractive ads from which you have had no response.

Checking the Classified Ads

For positions below $40,000, it will generally be worthwhile to check the classified section of Sunday papers under different key words. For example, if you were in the marketing field, you would obviously look under "marketing." However, you might also look under "advertising," "executive," "management," and "international." Many advertisers, especially the smaller firms, are not on target with their advertisements.

Answering Blind Advertisements

About 75% of all help-wanted advertisements are blind ads. These are ads which do not identify the advertiser. Blind advertisements are placed by executive search firms and corporations which are doing their own recruiting. Employment agencies are generally not permitted to run advertisements without identifying themselves.

These blind advertisements are usually placed for one of three reasons:

1.   A firm can avoid the burden of replying to all applicants, and will not be badgered by unwanted "phone call" and "walk-in" applicants.

2.   A blind advertisement permits a firm to maintain secrecy from both competitors and employees.

3.   Small firms and companies with a tarnished image can usually get more applicants if they use ads without their name.

You should be aware that some firms will run deceptive blind advertisements *(i.e. when no available position exists).* They may wish to simply gauge the market in terms of both numbers and quality. Sometimes they also scan the market in hopes of finding a replacement for a marginal employee.

This type of ad can sometimes trap a person into responding to his own company. More than a handful of people have made this mistake!

While blind advertisements can present problems, they can also give the alert job hunter an advantage he will not have on a company-identified advertisement. This is because a blind ad by a major corporation will generally attract less than half the competition, and the quality of respondents drops sharply.

A way to gain an even better competitive advantage would be to attempt to *identify the companies* who were placing blind advertisements and then make a direct approach.

For example, a blind ad may say that the position is a financial job with a cosmetic firm in Southern Connecticut. You could then send letters to the Vice Presidents of Finance at all cosmetic firms in Southern Connecticut, and reduce the risk of being screened out by the company personnel department.

Timing Your Answer to Each Advertisement

The timing of your answers to advertised openings is also important. It is generally advisable to delay responding until seven to fourteen days after an ad has appeared. This is significant for a couple of reasons.

1. The response pattern to an advertisement which will draw 300 resumes and which appears on a Sunday, usually runs about as follows (assuming the firm is running an ad for a position in New York under their own name and address):

Sunday	(date the ad appears)
Monday	5 resumes received
Tuesday	55 resumes received
Wednesday	105 resumes received
Thursday	60 resumes received
Friday	20 resumes received
- Later	55 resumes received

    As you can see, a resume that arrives before the end of the first week runs a greater risk of being lost in the competitive shuffle.

2. Most companies rarely fill good positions in a hurry. People like to screen a number of candidates, and if you are interviewed after many others, the employer will be in a better position to act quickly.

This is true for executive positions because most employers go through a refinement process in which they change their ideas about the type of individual they are seeking. Then, as time goes on, they become more anxious to fill a given position.

Obviously, there are exceptions to this, and for lower-level jobs this strategy does not apply.

Using a Letter Rather than a Resume

People who must sift through many resumes tend to screen out non-qualifiers. This is a very critical point. Since resumes provide more facts and history, they can work against you in this situation. When answering ads, my preferred approach is to make use of a strong letter, one that is targeted at the likely requirements for success in the advertised position.

Providing Financial Information

Recruitment ads often request information on salary history and objectives. In most cases, if you are at a relatively low salary, you obviously do not want to be excluded from consideration because of present earnings. In other cases, salary objective is a secondary consideration.

In the course of seeing individuals handle financial disclosure in every possible way, I've concluded that if you follow the guidelines below, you will maximize the rate at which you get interviews.

1. If you're seeking a position at less than $25,000, you should normally provide the information requested. However, if the ad does not request salary history or objectives, then you should not volunteer it.

2.   If you are seeking a position in the $25,000 to $45,000 range, you should submit only salary objective information. You should state it in the form of a broad range that is acceptable to you. You can indicate that a "starting" range is given because of the many other considerations which might affect your decision.

3.   If you are seeking a position above the $45,000 level, you should avoid disclosure of salary history or objectives.

This procedure may cause you concern about losing some opportunities. However, if you choose to comply with requests for financial information, you probably will find that your response from the ads you answer will be in the 1% to 2% range. In short, you will be ruled out on positions of interest which might otherwise have been negotiated.

There is another significant reason for non-compliance with these requests. If you are going to answer a lot of advertisements, especially blind ads, then broadcasting earnings or objectives may lead to some personal embarrassment. This information has a way of reaching people's friends, business associates, and even subordinates.

The key point to remember is that when an employer places an advertisement, he is spending his money to attract candidates. If he feels you have the right qualifications, he will be sure to contact you for whatever additional information he would like to have.

Follow Up on Advertised Openings

Plan a follow-up campaign on the most attractive advertisements you uncover. Your follow-up should be timed approximately three weeks after you first respond. Very few of your competitors will bother to demonstrate such initiative, and we've seen this produce results on many occasions. *(For example, the second time you answer an ad, send different materials, such as a cover letter and resume, instead of a letter.)*

Concluding Comments on Answering Ads

If you conscientiously apply the advice in this section, you will greatly improve the rate at which you develop interviews. However, remember that the help-wanted pages are basically an exchange place for resumes. The competition is very great, and the response you receive may be relatively low.

In selecting ads to answer, be sure to take a broad approach rather than limiting your response to situations where your qualifications match the requirements. Also, you should answer blind ads, although if you can identify an advertiser, you will do better by using a direct approach.

When you answer ads, you will do best if you send a letter which is tailored to the likely requirements for success in the position. Our second choice would involve sending a cover letter and resume.

Your replies should be on a delayed time schedule, and you should be sure to follow up on the most attractive ads. If you are just beginning your campaign, you should also definitely go back and answer all interesting ads which might have appeared during the previous 10 weeks or so.

Just to give you an idea of the job market competition, we have reproduced the statistics below from the replies to a blind ad for **Junior and Senior Marketing and Financial Executives.** *It was an eighth of one page in size and appeared in the Business Section of The New York Times. The ad was general, but attractive in terms of growth potential and compensation. There was, however, no indication of actual compensation, the nature of the industry or the location.*

Number of Total Responses		842
From New York Area		496
Outside of New York Area		346
Age:	*Under 25*	14
	25 - 29	126
	30 - 34	152
	35 - 39	169
	40 - 44	153
	Over 45	64
	Not Stated	164
Degrees:	*Bachelors*	501
	Masters	230
	Ph.D.	29
	All Others	82
Sent Resumes		807
Sent Resumes on 8½x11 White Paper		782
Sent Resumes Without Typed Cover Letter		161
Sent Letters Without Resume		35
Earnings:	*Under $10,000*	5
	10,000 - 14,999	71
	15,000 - 19,999	91
	20,000 - 24,999	181
	25,000 - 29,999	105
	Over $30,000	89
	Not Stated	300
Employed		702
Unemployed		56
Could Not Identify		84

CHAPTER 6

Placing Advertisements for Yourself

Every week there are thousands of individuals who place advertisements in newspapers in an effort to attract potential employers. Nevertheless, if you are operating without professional help, our experience indicates that placing ads will be a rather fruitless method for generating interviews.

In a survey conducted among 1,000 job hunters, I found only one individual who actually accepted a position through an interview resulting from an ad. However, a surprising number of people had placed advertisements and most felt they had wasted their money.

The people who placed advertisements often received answers from small employment agencies, along with letters offering career testing and low-cost resume writing. Many of the people surveyed did receive responses from smaller companies. However, most of the time this interest waned when the candidates revealed their salary objectives. Of course, there are exceptions and some people land jobs through placing ads. However, professional copywriting and large ad expenditures are usually required.

The Cost of "Position Wanted" Ads

"Position wanted" advertisements can be placed in almost any newspaper, trade magazine, or specialized business publication. The cost of space depends upon the circulation and type of audience.

The media which do the largest volume of business in "position wanted" advertising are the Sunday editions of major metropolitan newspapers. In the case of most large papers, a person can place an advertisement either in the classified section or in the business pages.

The classified sections are generally much less expensive than the latter. For example, a one-inch by one-column advertisement in the classified section of *The New York Sunday Times* costs approximately $50. A display advertisement of the same size in the business section would cost approximately $125. (As a general rule figure on getting a maximum of 12 lines per inch and an average of 5 words per line.)

The most popular national vehicle for this type of advertising is *The Wall Street Journal.* Their charge for a one-inch by one-column ad in their classified section (The Mart) is approximately as follows: Nationwide $320; Eastern Edition $122; Midwestern Edition $100; Western Edition $62; and Southwestern Edition $36.

Many of the nation's thousands of trade magazines carry "position wanted" ads. If you need a list of their names and addresses, you can generally research them in most libraries.

Display Ads vs. Classified Ads

"Position wanted" classified advertising offers a potential value only for the people who seek less than $20,000. Even then a potential exists primarily for people in rather specialized occupations (e.g., specific types of engineers, accountants, etc.).

Large companies usually don't bother watching the classified for "position wanted" notices. However, on occasion, an unusual requirement for a very specialized type of talent will prompt even a large employer to look in this direction. It is the smaller companies with limited recruiting budgets that sometimes regularly check these advertisements.

I have had occasion to see some higher level executives succeed with large display advertisements. I also know of a number of people who have had fairly good results from three-inch by two-column advertisements. Occasionally people have succeeded with a series of small display ads which were placed among the recruitment display ads.

If you are seeking a position above $50,000 and want to experiment with a display advertisement, *I suggest you skip the employment sections of newspapers.* You will experience your best results if you place a display ad in the most widely read section of the business pages. In terms of placement, you will find that the top right-hand corner of a newspaper page will give you maximum exposure.

A Technique For Avoiding Trial and Error

If you feel you must try one advertisement for yourself, I strongly urge that you first do some research. Take a look at the "position wanted" ads placed by people approximately one month ago. Pick out what you feel is the best ad that is similar to what you have in mind.

You should then send the individual who ran the ad a short note and ask if the ad was successful. Be sure to enclose a self-addressed and stamped envelope for the person's reply, along with a few dollars for his trouble.

Concluding Comments on Placing Ads

If you are seeking more than $25,000, you will require quite a bit of luck to make this type of investment worthwhile. If you do want to run an ad, try to select a newspaper or magazine that will be read by a large number of individuals you hope to reach.

If you are in a specialized occupation, consider using an ad in a special convention magazine in your field. If you have decided to place an ad in a major newspaper, I suggest you consider placing an ad in an area outside of the employment section. In any case, your best insurance would be to do careful research.

If you are seeking under $25,000, and if you are a specialist, you can consider using the classified section of your metropolitan paper. It is less expensive and you could employ the same research technique prior to spending your money. Of course, whether you are seeking a relatively low or high salary, I suggest you thoroughly explore other avenues before you place advertisements for yourself.

Major U.S. Newspapers Which You Might Consider for "Position Wanted" Advertising

Note: *The circulation listed is the approximate Sunday circulation.*
The asterisk symbol (*) means daily circulation.

		SUNDAY CIRCULATION
ALABAMA	Birmingham News Post Herald	
	2200 Fourth Ave. N., Birmingham, AL 35202	207,000
ARIZONA	Phoenix Republic Gazette	
	120 E. Van Buren, Phoenix, AZ 85004	370,000
	Tucson Star, Tucson Newspapers Inc.,	
	4850 S. Park Ave., Tucson, AZ 85726	129,000
ARKANSAS	Little Rock Arkansas Gazette	
	112 W. Third Ave., Little Rock, AK 72203	158,000
CALIFORNIA	Fresno Bee	
	1626 E. St., Fresno, CA 93786	146,000
	Long Beach Independent Press	
	604 Pine Ave., Long Beach, CA 90844	135,000
	Los Angeles Times	
	Times-Mirror Square, Los Angeles, CA 90053	1,307,000
	Orange County Bulletin	
	232 S. Lemon St., Anaheim, CA 92805	*13,221
	Orange County Star Progress	
	600 S. Palm St., La Habra, CA 90631	242,000
	Santa Ana Register	
	625 N. Grand Ave., Santa Ana, CA 92711	240,000
	Sacramento Bee	
	21st and Q Sts., Sacramento, CA 95816	210,000
	San Diego Union Tribune	
	350 Camino de la Reina, San Diego, CA 92108	329,000
	San Francisco Chronicle	
	925 Mission St., San Francisco, CA 94103	669,000
	San Jose Mercury News	
	750 Ridder Park Dr., San Jose, CA 95190	260,000
	Wall Street Journal (Western Edition)	
	1701 Page Mill Road, Palo Alto, CA 94304	*377,000
COLORADO	Denver Post	
	650-15th St., Denver, CO 80201	354,000
CONNECTICUT	Hartford Courant	
	285 Broad St., Hartford, CT 06115	287,000
DELAWARE	Wilmington News Journal	
	831 Orange St., Wilmington, DE 19899	106,000
D.C.	Washington Post	
	1150 15th St., N.W., Washington, D.C. 20071	820,000
FLORIDA	Fort Lauderdale News	
	101 N. New Riv. Dr. E., Ft. Laud., FL 33302	176,000
	Jacksonville Times Union	
	1 Riverside Ave., Jacksonville, FL 32231	206,000
	Miami Herald News	
	1 Herald Plaza, Miami, FL 33101	546,000

FLORIDA	Orlando Sentinel Star 633 N. Orange Ave., Orlando, FL 32802	220,000
	St. Petersburg Times 490 First Ave., St. Petersburg, FL 33701	263,000
	Tampa Tribune 202 S. Parker St., Tampa, FL 33601	224,000
GEORGIA	Atlanta Journal P.O. Box 4689, Atlanta, GA 30302	509,000
HAWAII	Hawaii Star Bulletin 605 Kapiolani Blvd., Honolulu, HI 96801	201,000
ILLINOIS	Chicago Tribune 435 N. Michigan Ave., Chicago, IL 60611	1,144,000
	Wall Street Journal (Midwest Edition) 200 W. Monroe St., Chicago, IL 60606	*465,000
INDIANA	Indianapolis Star News 307 N. Pennsylvania St., Indianapolis, IN 46206	357,000
IOWA	Des Moines Register Tribune 715 Locust St., Des Moines, IA 50309	402,000
KANSAS	Wichita Eagle Beacon 825 E. Douglas Ave., Wichita, KS 67202	174,000
KENTUCKY	Louisville Courier Journal & Times 525 W. Broadway, Louisville, KY 40202	335,000
LOUISIANA	New Orleans Times Picayune 3800 Howard Ave., New Orleans, LA 70140	319,000
MAINE	Portland Maine Sunday Telegram P.O. Box 1460, Portland, ME 04104	117,000
MARYLAND	Baltimore Sun 501 N. Calvert St., Baltimore, MD 21203	368,000
MASS.	Boston Globe 135 Morrissey Blvd., Boston, MA 02107	681,000
MICHIGAN	Detroit News 615 Lafayette Blvd., Detroit, MI 48231	824,000
MINNESOTA	Minneapolis Star Tribune 425 Portland Ave., Minneapolis, MN 55488	612,000
MISSISSIPPI	Jackson Clarion-Ledger 311 E. Pearl St., Jackson, MS 39205	117,000
MISSOURI	Kansas City Times 1729 Grand, Kansas City, MO 64108	403,000
	St. Louis Post-Dispatch 900 N. Tucker Blvd., St. Louis, MO 63101	436,000
NEBRASKA	Omaha World Herald World-Herald Square, Omaha, NE 68102	279,000
NEW JERSEY	Bergen Record 150 River Rd., Hackensack, NJ 07602	209,000
	Newark Star Ledger Star Ledger Plaza, Newark, NJ 07101	569,000

NEW MEXICO	Albuquerque Journal	
	717 Silver Ave., S.W., Albuquerque, NM 87103	123,000
NEW YORK	Albany Times Union	
	645 Albany-Shaker Rd., Albany, NY 12212	149,000
	Buffalo Courier Express	
	795 Main St., Buffalo, NY 14240	256,000
	Newsday	
	235 Pinelawn Rd., Melville, NY 11747	553,000
	New York Times	
	229 W. 43rd St., New York, NY 10036	1,415,000
	Rochester Democrat	
	55 Exchange St., Rochester, NY 14614	231,000
	Syracuse Herald-American	
	Clinton Square, Syracuse, NY 13221	237,000
	Wall Street Journal (Eastern Edition)	
	22 Cortlandt St., New York, NY 10007	*710,000
N. CAROLINA	Charlotte Observer News	
	600 S. Tryon St., Charlotte, NC 28232	238,000
	Raleigh News & Observer Times	
	215 S. McDowell St., Raleigh, NC 27602	163,000
OHIO	Akron Beacon Journal	
	44 E. Exchange St., Akron, OH 44328	217,000
	Cincinnati Enquirer	
	617 Vine St., Cincinnati, OH 45201	288,000
	Cleveland Plain Dealer	
	1801 Superior Ave., N.E., Cleveland, OH 44114	453,000
	Columbus Dispatch	
	34 S. Third St., Columbus, OH 43216	341,000
	Dayton News-Journal Herald	
	4th & Ludlow Sts., Dayton, OH 45401	263,000
	Toledo Blade Times	
	541 Superior St., Toledo, OH 43660	208,000
OKLAHOMA	Oklahoma City Oklahoman Times	
	Box 25125, Oklahoma City, OK 73125	287,000
	Tulsa World Tribune	
	315 S. Boulder, Tulsa, OK 74102	207,000
OREGON	Portland Oregonian-Oregon Journal	
	1320 S.W. Broadway, Portland, OR 97201	413,000
PENNSYLVANIA	Harrisburg Patriot News	
	812 Market St., Harrisburg, PA 17105	156,000
	Philadelphia Inquirer	
	400 N. Broad St., Philadelphia, PA 19101	846,000
	Pittsburgh Press	
	34 Blvd. of the Allies, Pittsburgh, PA 15230	661,000
RHODE ISLAND	Providence Journal	
	75 Fountain St., Providence, RI 02902	222,000
S. CAROLINA	Charleston Post News	
	134 Columbus St., Charleston, SC 29402	95,000
	Columbia State Record	
	Box 1333, Stadium Rd., Columbia, SC 29202	136,000
TENNESSEE	Memphis Commercial Appeal	
	495 Union Ave., Memphis, TN 38101	285,000

TENNESSEE	Nashville Tennessean	
	1100 Broadway St., Nashville, TN 37202	243,000
TEXAS	Dallas News	
	Communications Center, P.O. Box 225237,	
	Dallas, TX 75222	341,000
	Dallas Times Herald	
	1101 Pacific Ave., Dallas, TX 75202	336,000
	Fort Worth Star-Telegram	
	400 W. 7th St., Forth Worth, TX 76102	244,000
	Houston Chronicle	
	801 Texas Ave., Houston, TX 77001	428,000
	Houston Post	
	4747 S.W. Freeway, Houston, TX 77001	383,000
	San Antonio Express News	
	Ave. E and 3rd St., San Antonio, TX 78205	182,000
	San Antonio Light	
	P.O. Box 161, San Antonio, TX 78291	182,000
	Wall Street Journal (Southwest Edition)	
	1233 Regal Row, Dallas, TX 75247	*200,000
UTAH	Salt Lake City Desert News Tribune	
	143 S. Main St., Salt Lake City, UT 84110	179,000
VIRGINIA	Norfolk Virginia Beach Pilot	
	150 W. Brambleton Ave., Norfolk, VA 23501	202,000
	Richmond News-Leader Times Dispatch	
	333 E. Grace St., Richmond, VA 23219	214,000
WASHINGTON	Seattle Post-Intelligencer	
	6th & Wall Sts., Seattle, WA 98121	232,000
	Seattle Times	
	Fairview Ave., N.&JohnSts.,Seattle,WA 98111	340,000
	Spokane Chronicle Review	
	926 Sprague Ave., W., Spokane, WA 99201	121,000
	Tacoma News Tribune	
	Box 11000,Tacoma, WA 98411	107,000
W. VIRGINIA	Charleston Gazette Mail	
	1001 Virginia St., E., Charleston, WV 25330	107,000
WISCONSIN	Madison Wisconsin State Journal	
	P.O. Box 8056, Madison, WI 53708	125,000
	Milwaukee Journal Sentinel	
	333 W. State St., Milwaukee, WI 53201	533,000

CHAPTER 7

Direct Mail to Employers

A Fast Way to Get Interviews

I have found that the most consistently effective way for anyone to generate interviews is through direct mail to executives. This can work regardless of whether you are a graduating student, a female lawyer, a returning military officer, an engineer, an unemployed sales manager or a corporate officer.

The basic reason that direct mail can work so well is that you can project your best image, avoid initial disclosure of any liabilities, and make independent contact that is free from competition.

This method for generating interviews also offers the best potential for enabling you to either change careers or gain a position at a significant increase in earnings. With direct mail you can pick any field and contact top individuals who have the authority to offer attractive compensation.

Perhaps the most useful aspect of direct mail is that it can serve to uncover job opportunities that did not previously exist. If you address your campaign to senior executives and sufficiently impress them in an interview, they may search for a way to bring you aboard.

The top management of most organizations are well aware of the expenses involved with recruiting. When someone good comes to their attention, they can act rapidly to create a job situation. This may involve the development of a new position, or the shifting of someone of lesser competence in order to make room. In any event, every day people in all occupations are winning positions created under these circumstances.

Who to Contact

Your objective here is to contact top executives in those organizations which may have a need for your services. If you are seeking a position under $25,000, you can consider the use of mailings addressed to the Vice President of Personnel. Beyond this income range you will have to make use of personally addressed letters.

Contact Senior Executives

If you are seeking a salary *between $25,000 and $50,000*, I recommend that you consider directing your campaign to the Senior Vice President in charge of your specific functional area. I generally suggest that anyone above the $25,000 level avoid personnel departments. In almost all cases, the personnel office will not be doing the hiring, and you may just be placing one more obstacle in your path.

If you are seeking *more than $50,000*, your campaign should normally be aimed at one of the three top executives of the organizations in which you have an interest.

Directories which contain the addresses of companies and their corporate officers are listed at the end of the book, and are available in most large libraries. If you have a specific geographic preference, I suggest you call the business office of your local telephone company for free copies of both the white and yellow page phone books.

If you are a senior executive who must direct his mailing campaign to chief executive officers of America's largest corporations, a two-step mail effort is usually in order.

In these cases, the purpose of the initial contact is simply to generate a response from any individual who might be responsible for hiring you.

For example, CEO's in large firms rarely do initial screenings, even of top people. In most situations, an Executive VP, VP Personnel or other close associate will have the responsibility for initial contact with candidates for senior positions.

For contacting CEO's, a letter is preferable. Your reply, even a form reject, may come from the CEO's associate who should then become your target. Then, a few weeks after the reject, you should send a cover letter and resume to this individual and follow up via phone. These second-stage mailings are far more effective than initial mailings to CEO's.

Contact Recently Promoted Executives

I have also found that job seekers *contacting recently promoted people* have been consistently able to generate very useful leads. Your source for getting names would be from the press releases appearing in the business papers, trade magazines, and the business sections of the major newspapers.

The reason these people are such good prospects is that they often prefer to recruit their own new teams from the outside.

If you are at the executive level, the scanning of promotion announcements can offer you one other advantage. Quite frequently they provide the name of the former employer, and more often than not, the job they formerly occupied is still open.

Contact Alumni From Your College

You may also want to consider directing letters to *successful people who graduated from your college*. You probably have access to alumni directories which indicate positions and companies, or can find some alternative source for identifying successful graduates. In some cases, your letter should go to the home address of these people.

The letter you write should refer to your mutual interest in the college and solicit their assistance. Most of the time you will receive a warm and genuinely interested response.

The Size of a Direct Mail Campaign

When you execute a direct mail campaign, you will only generate a small percentage of interviews from the correspondence you initiate. This is a critical point. I say this because there is a great futility in the way many job seekers scatter resumes and evaluate the results.

Once you have prepared good materials, I suggest you execute a small test mailing to your prime audience. This will give you insight as to the probable effectiveness of a larger mailing. In most cases, the more letters you can afford to send out, the more opportunities you will have to explore. *Remember, however, that everything will depend on your having proper targets and superior materials . . . otherwise your investment here may be disappointing.*

There are certain specialized occupations in which job seekers have a limited number of potential employers. For example, musicians, educators, broadcasters, airline pilots, etc. If this is your situation, I suggest that you avoid making any initial contact with a resume. Your campaign will be most effective if it is based upon relatively long but well-written letters. I mean letters which may be two full pages in length.

If you have a limited number of opportunities, it is even more imperative that your campaign be launched in the most precise manner possible. In some situations, it is possible to generate an unusually high percentage of positive responses.

For example, recently I had occasion to assist a very marketable 33-year-old scientist who was earning $30,000. Forty key targets were identified, and á carefully tailored letter was forwarded to each company. He then followed up each letter with a phone call to request an interview. Offers for interviews were ultimately received from 23 of the organizations.

The Type of Letter to Use

The letter you use can either be in the form of a cover letter, which you would attach to your resume, or even more desirable a *personal letter* that would stand on its own merits. I have included some successful examples in a separate section of this book. Depending on your circumstances, you can consider the use of any one of five basic types of letters. For example you can have:

1. Letters which summarize your past experience and work history;

2. Letters which emphasize your previous accomplishments;

3. Letters which emphasize what happened as a result of your presence in an organization;

4. Letters which emphasize what you can do, and the results you can produce; or

5. Letters which were written in a curiosity-arousing style and which also borrow from the above types of letters.

There is no particular style of letter which is going to automatically be right for any individual. My experience has been that letters combining elements of the types described in (2) and (4) are usually good for most people. By the way, letters should never be sent out on your employer's letterhead. Use your own personal stationery.

The Response You Can Expect

The range of responses you will receive to your initial mailing will include the following:

1. A letter, phone call or telegram requesting that you call the firm;

2. A letter asking you to send more information; to complete an application form; or to send a detailed resume;

3. A polite rejection letter which will normally contain the statement that your resume will be kept in the active files;

4. No response at all.

As a general rule, the lower your position objectives, the higher the response you can expect from your mailing.

On the basis of having seen thousands of mail campaigns by people at all levels, we developed the following response criteria for large scale mailings in business occupations of average demand.

1. Under $25,000, you should look for a 6% to 8% positive response.

2. In the $25,000 to $50,000 range, a 3% to 4% positive response is good.

3. Above the $50,000 level, a 2% positive response is reasonable.

By positive response, I am referring to *any favorable inquiry* over a four to six-week period. This may take the form of a request for further information, a telephone discussion, or an immediate request for an interview.

For example, let us assume you are at $60,000, and that you have done a mailing to the Vice Presidents of Sales at *Fortune's* 1,000 largest industrial firms. I am saying that if in a four to six-week period, 20 companies (2%) express an interest in meeting you, you will have done quite well.

Of course, with this degree of interest, you should be able to nail down a few good job offers. As for the rest of the 1,000, about 250 will never even acknowledge your correspondence, and 730 will send you some form of a rejection letter.

The main point you need to appreciate is that because of the low positive response rate, the need for precise execution is paramount. There is a range of variables to consider, and a seemingly small drop in effectiveness can ruin your whole mail campaign. Obviously, a prime factor in anyone's success rate is the general demand for his profession at the time of his search. However, I have found that the quality of your materials is equally significant.

Direct Mail and Letter Guidelines

As a result of our experience in advising on direct mail job campaigns, we have established the following guidelines regarding technique.

1. A mailing to individuals by name will outpull a mailing addressed by title alone.

2. A mailing consisting of an individualized (tailored) letter will almost always outpull a mailing which consists of a form cover letter and a resume.

   (This does not mean that everyone should always use a letter, rather than a cover letter and a resume. More on this in the resume section.)

3. A mailing which utilizes Monarch size stationery (7¼" x 10½") represents a more personal style of communication and is preferred in many forms of correspondence.

4. Mailings with stationery (and resume) printed on any light shade or color of paper seem to do slightly better than the same materials printed on white bond stock. However, the use of strong colors will always lower your response.

5. A mailing to chief executives with envelopes marked "private and confidential" or "private and personal" will always outpull a mailing without these notations.

Some other rules of thumb for maximizing your direct mail effectiveness include the following:

1. When writing letters, always keep your sentences short and simple. Avoid the use of flowery words, be direct and to the point.

   Keep the paragraphs short — no more than five or six lines. Indenting the first line of each paragraph also seems to help improve readability.

2. If you are seeking an executive position and resort to mimeographed materials, you may be very disappointed with your results. People in lower salary ranges are an exception to this rule.

3. When contacting employers avoid the use of form letters where you type the name and address of an individual in a specific spot.

   If it doesn't match the rest of the letter, the individuals you contact will think you are trying to put something over on them.

4. If you have a means to get them typed, don't hesitate to use longer letters. These are most appropriate in carefully researched situations.

   In a mass campaign, the ideal length for a letter which is being sent by itself, is one page.

5. Sign your name with a blue felt tip pen. There is some indication that response is helped by the implication of forcefulness which these pens seem to give.

6. Avoid too much showmanship and materials which are too bold in appearance. The best letters are the ones of the soft-sell variety.

   Overselling can be just as disastrous as underselling. This is because you leave the reader with an impression of "If this guy is so good, why does he have to try so hard?"

7. Do not begin a letter by asking for a job. Letters which say, "I am looking for a job and wonder if you have any suitable opportunities" rarely work!

   Focus on your ability to meet the needs of the person you are writing. Communicate your achievements in a way that will make apparent the benefits you can bring an employer.

8. A good technique when writing a stranger is to say you have some "ideas" or "knowledge" that can benefit the organization. You should then offer to share the knowledge in a personal meeting.

9. If you have industry experience, be sure to mention it in the early part of your letter. If you do not have industry experience, then state

that you have always had an interest in the firm or its industry.

10. Where possible, use the names of both the firm and the individual in the body of your letter. Also, sign letters with your full name. The use of initials can cause some people to react negatively.

11. When you've written a letter, read it out loud. If you stumble, or find you are changing parts of the letter as you read, it needs more work. If you lose your breath, your sentences are too long. When you have a good letter, it will read smoothly and sound right to you.

12. Avoid use of the term "job hunting," and stress career rather than job orientation. In addition, avoid any mention of either your present earnings or expected income in your first letter to an organization.

    Also, as a general rule, people do better when they don't try to explain "why" they are looking. (There are certain exceptions to both of these which are reviewed in a later section.)

13. Keep exact records of all of your direct mail efforts. Avoid the temptation to mail out 10 letters an evening. Instead, have all your materials prepared in advance, and subsequently mailed at about the same time.

    With the exception of holiday weekends, the best days to mail are on a Saturday or Sunday. This way they will normally reach the people between Tuesday and Thursday, which is the time they are most likely to be at their desk.

14. While there is no single way to write a letter, you should outline your letters before you write them. Also, there are certain words that do "sell." You should look at the examples at the back of the book and try to

borrow the phrases that might be effective for you.

The most persuasive letters are the ones that are alive, cheerful and enthusiastic, as well as personal, warm, and human. They "read" just like people "speak." They sound like they were written for just one person. Materials which are detached or cold never do as well, even though you may think they are professional.

15. Based upon my experience, there are certain times when a direct mail campaign is more effective. There is a definite seasonal nature, and it does not apparently relate to the published job market, or the amount of help-wanted advertising that appears each month.

January is the best month to launch a mail campaign, and June and July are the worst. For junior people, a mailing in June will bring about half the immediate response of the same mailing done in January. The chart below illustrates average experience by month, with January as a base of 100.

January	100	July	60
February	95	August	85
March	90	September	75
April	75	October	90
May	70	November	80
June	60	December	70

The Importance of Follow-up

If you do not hear from a firm in which you have a particular interest, it will be worth it for you to follow up after four weeks. In the follow-up letter you should restate your interest and mention the contribution you could make.

A key point to remember for every phase of your job search, is that a good follow-up plan will always bring results. In fact, you may wish to duplicate an entire mailing. By the way, if you do this, my experience indicates you will normally get about 80% of the number of positive responses generated by your first mailing.

Concluding Comments on Direct Mail

Direct mail can offer anyone the quickest method for generating interviews. It is by far the best approach if you are someone seeking a career change or large salary increase. When you design your plan, you should allow for every possible detail. In fact, as you progress in your campaign, you should be ready to make adjustments if your response is not as expected.

There are some major risks in using direct mail. It can be expensive. It also needs to be executed with great precision. For senior executives, professional copywriting helps, and can be an excellent investment.

Over time we have found that it is not uncommon for professionals at all levels to launch mail campaigns which fail. When this happens they typically lose confidence in their marketability. However, analysis usually determines that their failure stemmed from two factors. The first was poor target selection. By this I mean not contacting the right person in the right firm. The second common reason for failure was having poor creative materials. Remember, average letters and resumes will not work. Superior materials are a necessity.

CHAPTER 8

Employment Agencies

In the world of job changing, there is a great deal of confusion over the role of employment agencies. Years ago, agencies worked for job hunters, and people paid them a fee if they accepted a job through an agency's referral. In recent decades, this role shifted to one in which almost all agencies work exclusively for employers. Some distinguish their new role by advertising that they have listings for "fee-paid" positions.

Unfortunately, there are people who contact agencies because they think that the agency will counsel them objectively and market them into a new job. Of course, this is not the case. Before you approach any agency, I think you should have a clear understanding of what they are and how they operate.

An employment agency is an organization (or person) who solicits job listings directly from employers for the purpose of earning a referral commission. Employers give them specific information on job openings including the duties, experience required and income ranges. The employers in turn become obligated to pay the agency a commission if they hire someone based upon the agency's referral.

Many agencies take job listings from their employer clients over the telephone. For their own protection, some like to have job hunters sign a contract which obligates the individual if the employer fails to pay the agency.

Today, all agencies which handle white collar professional or managerial positions can be grouped into three separate classifications.

Single industry agencies are those firms which receive listings for available jobs within one industry. For example, they might be specialists in the publishing industry, the steel industry, or the supermarket industry.

The second category of agencies is the *functional agencies.* They also specialize, but concentrate along occupational lines. For example, there are agencies which are specialists in marketing, EDP, engineering, retailing, etc.

The third and most common classification covers those agencies which are *generalists.* They get assignments across a wide industry and career field spectrum.

Be Selective in Choosing Agencies

In choosing agencies, it is important to be as selective as possible. You need to determine which companies are most active in your specialty and have a good reputation in general. Unfortunately, you can only rely on what you are able to find out from other people's experience. Even then, a good agency for one person can be the least effective for another.

If you are unfamiliar with agencies in a given city, you should be able to get some information from the local newspaper. Some of them maintain a directory of advertisers, and personnel at the paper may be able to give you some qualitative direction. Despite licensing requirements, many agencies experience high turnover and are staffed with inexperienced people. Some job candidates have encountered situations where their resumes were so broadly scattered that both their privacy and reputation were jeopardized.

In every city there is usually a group of truly fine employment agencies. *Within the top agencies there are exceptional and experienced men and women with very broad contacts.* If you can locate them, they can be of invaluable assistance if you succeed in developing a friendly relationship. In working with agencies you should be frank and honest, but always project great confidence in your own worth. When you're in the most active stage of your job search, be sure to maintain contact and follow up regularly.

When to Contact Agencies

Our philosophy and system of executive job changing does not put heavy reliance on contacting agencies. This is because a relatively small percentage of all agencies are effective for positions over $50,000. However, if you're seeking up to this level, then once your campaign is underway, you should contact three to five of the best agencies in your area.

This procedure is the opposite of the approach taken by most executives. When they begin to look for a new job, one of the first things they normally do is register with agencies. The immediate result may be discouragement about their own earnings potential or ability to change industries or career field. This can stem from the nature of the agency business rather than a person's chances for obtaining better employment.

You must remember that agencies are working for employers, not job candidates. A good agency must work at building long-term relationships with organizations, and job candidates are here today and gone tomorrow. They must concentrate on placing the most easily marketed candidates. If you are available at a good price, almost any smart agency will work hard to place you. However, if a major financial increase is your goal, then your opportunities through agencies will be limited.

The reason I suggest you contact a number of agencies is that this will simply improve your chances of being submitted for jobs. It is generally quite unusual for firms to get exclusive job listings. Because of this, while one agency may refuse to send you to an employer, another may submit your qualifications immediately.

Another reason for multiple registration has to do with the fact that most agencies like to submit a group of candidates to an employer. This will be true regardless of an agency's apparent enthusiasm over your qualifications. The one thing you must avoid is any decision to "shotgun" your resume to dozens of agencies within one city. If you do not rapidly land a position, this practice can eliminate the chances you would have had through a select group of fine firms.

How to Contact Agencies

If you are seeking between $25,000 and $45,000, you should be able to explore positions and quickly line up interviews via phone. Afternoons are the best time to reach agencies. If you are below the $25,000 level, I suggest that you contact them by sending a cover letter and resume in answer to a specific listing. This way you will be less likely to spend excessive time finding out that they do not have any positions where you meet the requirements.

If possible, direct your correspondence by name to an individual, preferably *an officer of the agency.* When you send your materials, be sure to avoid having them arrive at the beginning of the week. Agencies are deluged with both mail and business at that time. Also *insist* that the agency contact you prior to distributing your resume (or facts about your availability) to any company. Once you have allowed sufficient time for your materials to reach the agency, you should then follow up by phone.

Agency Registration Forms

If you are between $25,000 and $50,000, and only interested in fee-paid positions, you should avoid completing too many agency forms. Completing the forms can be quite time-consuming. In addition, some agencies have high turnover and the personal information in their files may come back to haunt you.

At the higher salary ranges, agencies will probably not ask you to complete their application and sign their contract. However, if your letter does bring such a form in the mail, you should sign it, but refer them to your resume and indicate that you will consider fee-paid positions only.

To evaluate your qualifications, an agency may need a lot of specific facts about you. If your resume does not contain the complete information an agency needs, you should write the pertinent data they might require.

Listings of Major Employment Agencies

As previously indicated, I strongly urge that you do not contact agencies on a blind basis. It is also best to make contact in relation to a specific position which they have advertised.

However, for the benefit of individuals who are out of the United States, and for those who seek to relocate great distances, I have listed the agencies in charge of state chapters of the National Association of Personnel Consultants. These firms can supply you with the names and addresses of all members in their state.

National Association of Personnel Consultants
State Presidents

ALABAMA
George Barnes
Snelling & Snelling
1217 N. Memorial Parkway
Huntsville, AL 35801

ARIZONA
Mitchell Young
Mitchell & Associates
2450 S. 4th Avenue, #305
Yuma, AZ 85364

ARKANSAS
Devone Payne, CPC
Snelling & Snelling
1049 First National Bank Bldg.
Little Rock, AR 72201

CALIFORNIA
Robert Read
Sales Consultants
50 California St., 35th Fl.
San Francisco, CA 94111

CAPITAL AREA
Frank Grammatica
Ogilvie Associates
7777 Leesburg Pike
Falls Church, VA 22043

COLORADO
Joe Sweeney, CPC
Sweeney Consultants
6825 E. Tennessee, Suite 407
Denver, CO 80222

CONNECTICUT
Louis Hipp, III, CPC
Hipp Waters Associates
64 Greenwich Avenue
Greenwich, CT 06830

DELAWARE
Barry S. Schlecker
Barry Personnel
901 Washington Street
Wilmington, DE 19801

FLORIDA
Norman Floyd
Snelling & Snelling
1135 NW 23rd Avenue
Gainesville, FL 32601

GEORGIA
Betty M. Arnold
Arnold Personnel Services, Inc.
1945 The Exchange, #310
Atlanta, GA 30339

HAWAII
Harold Yokoyama, CPC
Associates Services Ltd.
1164 Bishop Street, #407
Honolulu, HI 96813

ILLINOIS
Hellen Dawson
Professional Employment, Inc.
5005 Newport Drive, #104
Rolling Meadows, IL 60008

INDIANA
L. Deane Shepard, CPC
Century Personnel
3737 N. Meridian St., #203
Indianapolis, IN 46208

IOWA
Mary A. Liggett, CPC
M.A. Liggett, Inc.
P.O. Box 1024
3625 Utica Ridge Road, #202
Bettendorf, IA 52722

KENTUCKY

Rachael Nelson
Employer's Personnel, Inc.
4010 Dupont Circle
Louisville, KY 40207

LOUISIANA

D. Cleveland Franklin, CPC
Management Recruiters
P.O. Box 14932
Baton Rouge, LA 70898

MASSACHUSETTS

Bernard Hirsch
Quality Personnel
339 Hancock
N. Quincy, MA 02171

MICHIGAN

Fred Hertz
Professional Personnel Consultants
19189 W. Ten Mile Road
Southfield, MI 48075

MINNESOTA

Ceil Kelly
Business Personnel, Inc.
2345 Rice Street, Suite 228
Roseville, MN 55113

MISSISSIPPI

Eddie Frith
Jackson Employment Service
633 N. State Street, #202
Jackson, MS 39202

MISSOURI

Allen Oldfield
Professional Career Development
7777 Bonhomme, #1326
Clayton, MO 63105

MONTANA

Roger Koopman
Career Concepts — Bozeman
2304 West Main, #8
Bozeman, MT 59715

NEBRASKA

John Naylor
Overland Wolf Center
6910 Pacific Street, #105
Omaha, NE 68106

NEW HAMPSHIRE

David J. Craig, CPC
Craig's Criterion, Inc.
160 South River Road
Bedford, NH 03102

NEW JERSEY

Jeffrey Ryan, CPC
Career Center Management
369 Passaic Avenue
Fairfield, NJ 07006

NEW YORK

Carl F. Denny, CPC
Carlden Personnel Services
10740 Queens Blvd.
New York, NY 11372

NORTH CAROLINA

Debbie Darr
Executive Resources
Wachovia Building, #1308
Winston-Salem, NC 27101

OHIO

Jack Richardson, CPC
Opportunity Consultants, Inc.
Tri-State Building, #208
432 Walnut Street
Cincinnati, OH 45202

OKLAHOMA

Margaret Wick
Wick Personnel
7030 South Yale, #410
Tulsa, OK 74117

OREGON

Brent Norman
Murphy, Symonds & Stowell
1001 SW Fifth Ave., #1110
Portland, OR 97204

PENNSYLVANIA

David Teeple
Action Personnel
737 Fox Pavilion
Jenkintown, PA 19046

RHODE ISLAND

Mary Shaw
New England Consultants
Howard Building, #718
10 Dorrance Street
Providence, RI 02903

SOUTH CAROLINA

Thelma Bridgeman
Atlas Personnel
465 East Kennedy St.
Spartanburg, SC 29302

TENNESSEE

William Rasmussen
Rasmussen Associates
904 Executive Park Drive, #130
Knoxville, TN 37919

TEXAS

Beverly Scott
Career Woman Personnel Consultants
1525 Elm Street, #2030
Dallas, TX 75201

UTAH

Dave Goodwill
Creative Employment Service
1325 S. Main Street, #201
Salt Lake City, UT 84115

VIRGINIA

Verna Falwell
Houston Personnel
2015 Wards Road
Lynchburg, VA 24502

WASHINGTON

Gary Maybee
Theresa Snow Recruiters
400-108th Avenue, NE, #108
Bellevue, WA 98004

WEST VIRGINIA

James West
Snelling & Snelling
1107½ Market Plaza
Wheeling, WV 26003

WISCONSIN

Allan Bley
Placements of Racine, Inc.
425 Main Street, Ste. 405
Racine, WI 53403

CHAPTER 9

Executive Search Firms

Executive search firms are most commonly called recruiters or head-hunters. They work for organizations which are seeking to hire executives; they do not work for individuals seeking jobs. When they are retained for a search, their assignment is to find and submit qualified candidates for the specific position which the employer has available.

The fees which search firms charge employers for their services usually range from 25% to 33% of the starting annual compensation on a given position. This is exclusive of all out-of-pocket expenses such as travel, lunches and advertising expenses. Once retained, they are paid regardless of whether they find a candidate which their client is willing to hire.

Most of the top search firms are respected companies with well-earned reputations. They have recruited many of the business leaders in both the United States and Europe. The individuals employed by the better firms are usually educated, articulate and polished. They include many senior people who have achieved earlier success in a broad range of management disciplines.

While there are hundreds of legitimate search firms, there are many companies which call themselves "search firms," but which are really employment agencies who work on a contingency basis. Some career counseling firms who work for individual job seekers also use the "search" label even though they do no real executive recruiting. This misleading practice exists because there are no licensing requirements which govern the recruiting business. Anyone with a private phone can claim he is a recruiter. As a job seeker, you should be wary of the counterfeits, or you may waste a lot of time.

The Major Firms

During the last decade, the search industry came of age. In fact, on October 9, 1978, *Fortune* magazine ran a cover story on the "Big Six" executive search firms, and then followed-up with a commentary in their September 7, 1981 issue. Nevertheless, this industry remains rather fragmented and includes a great many small firms throughout the U.S.

At the end of this chapter, you will find a brief listing of some of the larger firms which are active in executive search. While many are headquartered in New York City, they receive assignments from throughout the United States and Europe. Included in this listing are some management consultants and CPA firms which offer executive search as an auxiliary service.

I cannot provide you with a rank order listing of the size of these companies. However, among the very largest organizations are Korn/Ferry, Heidrick & Struggles, Russell Reynolds Associates, Spencer Stuart & Associates, Boyden Associates, and Egon Zehnder.

Within the executive recruiting industry there are also many other firms who enjoy considerable prestige and who often work on select high-level assignments. Many smaller firms are specialists with recruiting efforts that are focused within a few industries.

In the last decade, the growing demand for executive talent has accelerated the growth of companies in this field. Almost all Fortune 500 companies have used recruiters on some occasion, as well as thousands of smaller organizations with occasional needs for adding key executives.

During the early 1980's the executive search industry will probably account for between 1,200 and 1,600 placements each month (from 15,000 to approximately 19,000 on an annual basis). In addition to recruiting business executives, these statistics reflect the efforts search firms make across many disciplines, including their work to recruit scientists, university presidents, political staffers, union leaders, professional fund-raisers, etc.

How Search Firms Find Candidates

Recruiters have a preference for candidates who are achievers, who make a strong first impression, and who are successfully employed in other firms. These are the individuals who are most presentable to a recruiter's clients. Because of this, at the higher executive levels, individuals can be at a slight disadvantage when their availability is published.

Recruiters generally get the names of potential candidates from directories, articles in the press, and their own professional and business contacts. Some occasionally use blind advertisements in the "help-wanted" sections of newspapers. Their other major source for candidates is from their own files, as some of the larger firms maintain information on more than 50,000 individual executives.

On any given assignment, a recruiter may carefully screen many dozens of candidates, seeking four to six individuals who meet the profile the employer has specified. Those selected are referred to the employer for interviews. While the employer is making a decision as to who is preferred, the recruiter must generally work to sell all the candidates on the firm and the specific job assignment.

How You Should Contact Search Firms

If you are seeking a position above $30,000, I recommend that you contact executive search firms in the early part of your campaign. Because timing is critical, "luck" can play a significant role in your attempt to make use of search firms.

Your chance of reaching a company when they have an assignment for your specific background is slim.

In view of this, I suggest that your primary objective with recruiters should be to establish a favorable contact at an early stage. There will be many instances where recruiters call you months after they have first become acquainted with your qualifications.

Unfortunately, most large search firms are contacted by from 30-100 job seekers each day. About 35% do not acknowledge correspondence from individuals because of the expense involved. The better companies do screen their incoming mail and categorize attractive candidates for review.

The best relationships with recruiting firms are the ones that begin with their contacting you. Being visible in your industry is the key to success with recruiters. If you have been writing articles, giving speeches or have been the recipient of awards, you have probably been contacted by some of these firms. If you have kept track of the names of recruiters that have called you, one of the first things you should now do is to renew these associations.

If you are not in the select category of being visible, you will have to initiate action on a direct basis.

One way to accomplish this involves your obtaining the names of individuals in recruiting firms from friends and other job seekers. You could then contact these people and mention that your associates had suggested that you call them. This action on your part will normally result in the recruiter asking you to send a resume or inviting you directly for an interview.

Your second alternative is to make contact by mail. In this case, you are going to have to send a superior summary of your qualifications in letter form, or a good transmittal letter along with your resume.

The Resume Approach

If you have developed a superior resume, you may wish to distribute it with a cover letter to recruiters.

Under most circumstances, your initial correspondence should not provide search firms with your present earnings. While recruiters always prefer to have full information at their disposal, the preliminary disclosure of financial information is unprofessional and makes people seem too available. However, it is often appropriate to provide recruiters with minimum income requirements or a range that you would consider.

The response that you can expect from a mailing to search firms will vary with your personal marketability as well as your occupational field and industry. Our firm has managed the campaigns of all types of people, and we often put our clients in touch with hundreds of search firms. In business fields of average demand, we anticipate a positive response of about 4-6% over a six-week period.

The recruiters that are interested in you will either drop you a short note asking you contact them or will telephone you and request further information. By the way, if your correspondence fails to supply a telephone number which will be answered during normal business hours, you may lose a significant percentage of your leads.

The Letter Approach

The use of personalized letters will usually bring some-what more inquiries than a cover letter and resume approach. Unfortunately, it is more time consuming and expensive because of the amount of typing involved.

For people who are seeking to find a job quickly, I normally prefer the resume approach. As an alternative, you might choose to send letters to select firms, and use a resume and cover letter for contacting the majority.

The use of a letter enables executives with problem backgrounds to avoid disclosure of liabilities which may be apparent in their resume.

One technique in timing that you could consider would be to contact recruiters prior to your actual initiation of a full-scale campaign. For example, at the earliest stage you could send recruiters a note which indicates that during the upcoming months, you expect to explore new positions. Obviously, your letter would then have to provide the search firm with enough details to stimulate an interest.

This approach will pave the way for you to discreetly make a second contact at a later date. All of the replies to your initial mailing should be kept on file. When your campaign is in full force you could then contact the individuals who had previously reported to you.

Imaging Yourself with Search Firms

If you are a young executive, you should begin developing contacts with recruiters early in your career. Some will invite you to see them even when they don't have specific assignments. If you can afford the time to spend with them, it may help you in the future.

In your relationships with recruiters, you should be honest, while pursuing a soft sell and attempting to avoid having them view you as just another job hunter. If you appear desperate or too available, they may never recommend you to their clients.

In general, you will be most popular with recruiters if you are a person who will explore attractive situations, but who is not too unhappy with his current employer.

During interviews with recruiters, appearance and first impressions are of primary importance. Once a firm develops a negative impression, it may eliminate future opportunities through that firm.

Remember that a recruiter will never recommend you until he has had the opportunity to screen you in at least one interview. For high-level positions, some firms will have you screened by two members of their staff, and they may prefer to meet with you on several occasions.

As with any other personal marketing effort, your use of appropriate follow-up can be critical to your success. Once you have presented your qualifications to recruiters, be sure to follow up your initial contact within 90 to 120 days. Your follow-up action should make use of materials which are different from those which you initially distributed. For example, if your first campaign effort to recruiters utilized a one to two-page letter, then I suggest that your follow-up contact make use of a cover letter and resume.

As a summary comment on executive search firms, it is important that you recognize that recruiters will be primarily interested in individuals who are highly marketable, who have blue-chip backgrounds and who have industry knowledge that can quickly facilitate a major contribution to their employer clients.

Some of the Major Executive Search Firms

Antell, Nagel, Moorehead & Assoc.
230 Park Ave.
New York, NY 10017

David T. Barry Assoc., Inc.
572 Washington St.
Wellesley, MA 02181

Battalia, Lotz & Assoc. Inc.
342 Madison Ave.
New York, NY 10017

Billington, Fox & Ellis, Inc.
20 North Wacker Dr.
Chicago, IL 60606

Boyden Assoc., Inc.
260 Madison Ave./Suite 2000
New York, NY 10016

Thomas A. Buffum Assoc.
2 Center Plaza
Boston, MA 02108

Canny, Bowen, Inc.
425 Park Ave.
New York, NY 10022

William H. Clark Assoc., Inc.
330 Madison Ave.
New York, NY 10017

Dean Bauben Assoc.
P.O. Box 228
Lunenburg, MA 01462

Thorndike Deland Assoc.
1440 Broadway/Suite 2264
New York, NY 10018

Devoto & Berry Partners, Ltd.
120 S. Riverside Plaza
Chicago, IL 60606

Eastman & Beaudine, Inc.
111W. Monroe St./Suite 2150
Chicago, IL 60603

Einstein Assoc., Inc.
380 Lexington Ave.
New York, NY 10017

Gorden Edwards Assoc.
P.O. Box 204
Verona, NJ 07044

Gould & McCoy, Inc.
375 Park Ave.
New York, NY 10022

Haley Assoc., Inc.
375 Park Ave.
New York, NY 10152

Handy Assoc., Inc.
245 Park Ave.
New York, NY 10167

F.P. Healy & Co., Inc.
630 Third Ave.
New York, NY 10017

Heidrick & Struggles, Inc.
125 S. Wacker Dr./Ste. 2800
Chicago, IL 60606

Hergenrather & Co.
3435 Wilshire Blvd.
Los Angeles, CA 90010

Ward Howell International
99 Park Ave./20th Floor
New York, NY 10016

Korn/Ferry International
1900 Avenue of the Stars
Los Angeles, CA 90067

Kremple & Meade
1900 Avenue of the Stars
Los Angeles, CA 90067

Owen, Webb Associates, Inc.
280 Park Ave.
New York, NY 10017

Parker, Eldrige, Scholl & Gordon Inc.
440 Totten Pond Rd.
Waltham, MA 02154

Paul R. Ray & Co., Inc.
1208 Ridgelea St.
Fort Worth, TX 76116

Russell Reynolds Assoc., Inc.
245 Park Ave.
New York, NY 10167

John W. Siler & Assoc. Inc.
5261 N. Port Washington Rd.
Milwaukee, WI 53217

Spencer Stuart & Assoc.
500 N. Michigan Ave./Suite 300
Chicago, IL 60611

Staub, Warmbold & Associates, Inc.
655 Third Ave.
New York, NY 10017

Yelverton & Mace, Inc.
350 California St./Suite 1680
San Francisco, CA 94104

Arthur Young & Co.
Executive Search Division
277 Park Ave.
New York, NY 10017

Egon Zehnder International
645 Fifth Ave.
New York, NY 10022

CHAPTER 10

Professional Associations

There are many professional organizations, alumni groups and trade associations which act as intermediaries between job hunters and organizations. If you have the opportunity to make use of these organizations, I suggest that you investigate them early in your campaign.

In order to take advantage of their services, you don't have to be active in their organizations. Most of these groups operate as "resume clearing houses," and they rarely charge either the job hunter or a corporation a fee. In terms of potential effectiveness, there is a wide variation that is usually a reflection of the individual in charge.

In certain situations, it can be unwise to leave your resume with these groups. If you are in a delicate position, I suggest that you provide them with a resume which has no personal identification. Your basic resume, less your name, address and present employer should prove adequate.

This type of documentation just mentioned provides the information necessary to determine if your background matches someone's needs. Of course, if you know the director of an organization on a personal basis, you could arrange to have him reveal additional information (your employer and salary) at his discretion.

In general, I believe that alumni groups and professional organizations are most effective for young people, particularly recent graduates who are specialists, and who seek under $25,000. There are some organizations which can prove very effective for young individuals seeking up to $50,000. These are primarily the ones serving accountants, lawyers, engineers, and people in health or education.

The executive directors of associations, Chambers of Commerce, and fraternal organizations such as the Toastmasters International or Jaycees, usually have many "lines" into their business communities. They know where growth is occurring and may be aware of specific vacancies.

Most associations have internal committees which focus on specific action areas such as government relations, technical activities, trade shows, and sales promotion. Individuals leading these special groups frequently have awareness of existing job opportunities. To reach these committee chairmen, you would have to write to the association requesting a list of officers.

Any Chamber of Commerce office will usually maintain a list of local organizations whose leaders might be helpful in a job campaign. For example, in the Boston area there are 30 or more organizations with names such as the Massachusetts High Technology Council, Associated Industries of Massachusetts, Massachusetts International Business Association, etc. Leaders of any one of these groups could help you gain new contacts and awareness of specific openings in your field.

Trade or professional groups also fund and manage business magazines, journals, newsletters, membership lists, industry directories, trade show catalogs and numerous other publications. The editors, publishers and contributors to these journals are influential people you might consider contacting.

New products which generate new employment often appear in prototype form at trade shows. Exhibitor directories can provide a comprehensive list of companies in a given field and also provide names of key people to contact. Importantly, when high level individuals attend trade shows, they are usually in a receptive frame of mind.

The *Encyclopedia of Associations* is the primary resource for locating associations. It provides the name and address for each group, the top executive to contact, lists of publications, and descriptions of internal committees. Conventions/trade show dates with locations are indicated for one or two years into the future.

CHAPTER 11

Dramatic Approaches for Getting Interviews

During the course of your campaign, you might consider experimenting with some less common approaches for generating interviews. Creativity is so rarely displayed by job hunters that almost any offbeat approach can be quite effective if executed tactfully.

The Telephone

"Cold" phone contact can be costly and frustrating. However, it is a fast and direct method of reaching decision makers when circumstances are right. For example, if you are interested in the possibility of joining a competitor or closely allied firm, a personal phone call may be appropriate.

In other cases, you may use a phone follow-up system to back up a direct mail campaign. In fact, you will almost always improve your effectiveness by adding a notation to your letters such as, "I will phone you next Wednesday..." This can increase readability as well as motivate the recipient to set your materials aside in expectation of your call.

It is possible to make use of the phone as the entire base for a job campaign. What you need to do, of course, is to first get the names of just the right individuals to contact. The types of people you might consider calling include Vice Presidents of Personnel, Vice Presidents of your specific functional area (Marketing, Manufacturing, etc.) and/or company Presidents.

The problems which you will face in making cold calls to strangers are numerous. However, the main ones are that you will call people at the wrong time, or will be unable to get past their secretary. Unfortunately, good secretaries can provide an effective screen for executives, especially since you will not want to leave a message with them.

Nevertheless, in many cases you will find it surprisingly easy to reach people at all levels by phone. You will probably need to develop and practice your phone "presentation," something which effectively conveys that "it is imperative I speak to him."

When you do get through to the person you want, your main objective would be to gain an invitation for an interview. A second, less desirable alternative, would be to have them refer you to someone else. At the very least, you want them to request that you forward a resume for their review.

The best time to make contact with people is usually just after 5:00 P.M. At that time, the switchboard is often still open, many secretaries have departed, and the person you want may answer his own phone.

If calling people during the late hour just mentioned does not prove successful, you might consider doing the reverse. For example, calling a person before regular business hours, or just before or after the normal lunch hour.

Valuable assets for any phone campaign include a clear and strong phone presence, a tightly rehearsed presentation, lots of charm, and a tough skin when you catch someone at the wrong time.

To be effective in your efforts, it will also be necessary that you execute your phone campaign with both total confidence and persistence. The major negative associated with calling people is the cost. If it takes three or four long distance calls to reach each person, things can get quite expensive.

Telegrams

There is nothing quite like a telegram. This is because you can be sure your telegram will always be read. Since this is an expensive approach, I suggest you save this technique for answering an ad or contacting an executive in a company of special interest. In the telegram, you would briefly summarize your key qualifications and say that your resume, letter or phone call will follow shortly.

Special Delivery or Registered Letters

Another technique for insuring readership involves use of a special delivery or registered letter. Anything that arrives "registered" has a better chance of being read by the executive to whom it is addressed.

Newsletters

Another source you might investigate includes the editors and publishers of newsletters. The growth in popularity of newsletters has resulted in many hundreds of such publications being available. Some of them are carefully read by executives at all levels, including corporate presidents. In general, they seem to be enjoying a growing influence as outside communications sources.

The editors of newsletters will occasionally offer to act as an exchange medium between executives and employers seeking management talent. They are periodically informed of openings and will forward your resume if you seem to be the type of executive material the employer can use.

Other Rarely Used Approaches

There are many other approaches which young people have used to generate interviews. In general, the success of a dramatic approach depends on the exercising of good taste. Dramatic approaches will never work for upper management or top-level people. However, I know of some young people who have applied almost all the sales approaches commonly used in selling both products and services.

For example, this would include the use of brochures as well as stamped and self-addressed reply cards. Other people have had their resumes delivered by messenger services in envelopes marked "Rush and Personal."

Middle management people have successfully utilized communications with outsiders who are on a firm's Board of Directors. The partners in the major investment banking firms frequently sit on the Boards of many firms. Some of them like to suggest good talent and can be very receptive.

CHAPTER 12

Professional Services

The concept of professional help for job seekers is not a new one. However, during the late 1970's, the emergence of the executive marketing concept signaled a major advancement. The practical assistance now available is far more results-oriented than the career counseling services which have been around for many decades.

There are only a few firms engaged in executive marketing as we originally conceived it. One reason is that the staffing requirements are fairly rigorous.

In addition, substantial resources are required in order to be able to provide career planning and directional consulting; development of marketing plans; professional writing services; research on employers and job openings; and printing and administrative assistance. The management of executive job campaigns involves work in all these areas, as well as consulting from start to finish.

About Selecting Professional Help

For many years, some people have been skeptical about the career industry, and I believe rightly so. As with executive search, anyone can start a business in this field and claim to be a career expert. Also, the advertising practices of certain organizations have been misleading.

For example, some firms claim to have valuable relationships with employers which can benefit job seekers. This is rarely true and should be viewed with skepticism. Others advertise marketing capabilities when in reality they are only job or career counselors. You should understand that counseling firms simply provide advice.

As a client of a counselor, you would still have to do all of your own writing, research, printing and marketing.

At the same time, be wary of small or local firms that imply a broad capability. Regardless of what they may claim, they cannot possibly have the depth of talent or resources for assisting people from all fields.

Also, you should be careful about dealing with anyone who advertises or implies a guarantee. In these cases, the first thing you should do is find out what is being guaranteed. I can assure you there is no one in the world who can honestly guarantee another human being a job.

In any case, when you retain professional help, make sure you have an agreement that specifies exactly what the organizations will do for you. Also, most importantly, find out about their consumer protection policy. The reasons for considering professional assistance are reviewed below.

Understanding Your Potential

Many individuals do not recognize the importance of having clear and realistic goals. However, my own experience has been that for exceptional job search results, the establishment of proper career objectives is a necessity.

The truth is that it is often difficult for people to assess their own potential. Personal counseling is a vehicle which can definitely assist people in this regard. Professionals can help people plan their moves with a better picture of their strengths, as well as giving them communicative solutions for dealing with any liabilities. This usually includes some creative thinking on precisely what to say or not say about yourself in all job search communications.

Identifying Career and Industry Direction

Once a person's strengths, liabilities and personal goals are understood, some then have a tendency to define their opportunity areas in narrow terms.

In certain cases, notably with specialists, people mistakenly proceed on the assumption that they are locked into a given position or field. Others hold the notion that there are few opportunities open to them because they are generalists. The truth is, capable generalists are needed in almost every industry and the skills of a specialist are often far more transferable than generally understood.

A good professional firm should have a variety of experts familiar with all facets of the job market. They also should be able to identify those industries which are most likely to have the openings appropriate to your interest, talents and income needs.

Developing a Marketing Plan

To find and win the job that is right for you, you must understand the avenues for entering the job markets, and you should master the techniques for logically approaching each market segment.

For maximum effectiveness, a personal marketing plan should be developed before your job campaign is ever launched. The goal of the plan would be the generation of sufficient interview possibilities, and should cover "what" you should do . . . and "how" . . . "when" . . . and "where" you should do it. In essence, this is no different than a marketing plan which a company would prepare before launching a new product.

In this regard, a professional can structure a complete personal action program for you, including exactly what you must do in each channel of activity. By leaving nothing to chance, assistance of this type can often help people generate far more interviews and save them from a lot of frustrating trial and error

Writing Resumes and Letters

Writing superior material about yourself can be one of the most difficult tasks imaginable. The greater your depth of experience, the more difficult this task can become.

Professional copywriting is an increasingly popular solution for individuals in all disciplines. Company presidents, theatrical people and political figures have had copywriters work with them for years. Today, executives and professionals are doing the same thing in order to compete for the most attractive jobs.

Researching the Job Markets

In order to launch a job campaign, you need to have specific targets. The names of most of the employers and recruiters for you to contact should be developed in advance. Additionally, it is wise to stay abreast of openings that come on the published job markets in all geographic areas of interest.

To assist job seekers in dealing with the published job market, our firm has developed a capacity for reviewing all major newspapers and magazines on a daily basis. What we do is to summarize for our clients, in digest form, all of the professional, managerial and executive openings which are advertised.

As previously mentioned, most employers also have openings which are not published. For the most part, these jobs can only be discovered through direct contact with the organizations which have the openings.

In this area, computers can be used to identify the right organizations for a person to contact . . . according to a person's preferences for location, employer size and type of industry.

Research assistance can save hundreds of hours of work. Whether it's appropriate to consider depends upon the extent of the job campaign that is required.

Developing Interviewing Skills

Many people assume there is little they can do to prepare for interviews. Nothing could be further from the truth. The smartest job seekers are very well prepared. They know how to control the pace and direction of interviews, and are experts at projecting an appropriate image.

The most effective consultants in this area usually cover the development of a basic communications strategy for the individual to implement in all interviews. A good plan, combined with a little practice interviewing, can give an incredible boost to anyone's skills.

Assessing your needs for this kind of help can be a very simple matter. If you are converting a high percentage of interviews into offers, you may already be masterful. If the reverse is true, then professional assistance may be a necessity.

Administrative and Marketing Support

There are many details involved in launching a job campaign. Some individuals prefer to avoid the headaches of the administrative work load. The details I am referring to here include such matters as varityping of resumes, paper selection, printing of resumes, letterhead and envelopes, as well as the typing of letters, campaign mailings, etc. The more sophisticated firms offer this type of support.

The Emergence of Outplacement as a Major Severance Benefit

Firing anyone is never pleasant. In fact, it usually involves an emotionally charged and very unpleasant situation. For this reason, termination decisions are often delayed as long as possible . . . and in many companies these deferrals can be a costly mistake for all concerned.

Now, however, Outplacement Consultants are using the executive marketing concept to make the task and the decision a lot easier. There is little doubt that it offers the most practical, moral and economic way for management to deal with the sensitive issue of staff reduction.

In essence it involves marketing people into satisfactory new jobs and is used increasingly in mergers, reorganizations, cutbacks and individual terminations. Our own firm, Performance Dynamics International, is the pioneer of the Outplacement Marketing concept. As such, we have served large and small employers from throughout the country who have had us market departing personnel into productive new jobs.

During the latter 1970's, this concept enjoyed growing acceptance. During the 1980's, it is likely to become a regular benefit which is available to managers, professionals and executives at all levels. In fact, most of the country's leading employers already provide some form of services to all key executive personnel.

The cost to corporations for outplacement marketing services ranges from 10 to 20% of the terminated individual's compensation (annual salary at the time of termination plus most recent annual bonus).

Outplacement counseling programs (which are less complete) are available at fees which are usually 10% or less. These are usually similar to career counseling services, and are only educational and advisory in their thrust. They do not include copywriting, research, marketing or administrative support.

What does outplacement marketing mean to terminated employees?

It means that they can . . . with dignity and the ability to maintain goodwill towards their former employers . . . continue productive careers, most often without incurring loss of respect or income to their families.

What does it mean to the managers who must do terminations?

The knowledge that employees will be professionally assisted and moved into new jobs, eliminates the concerns which delay most termination decisions. With this knowledge, managers can approach difficult issues with good conscience, and can move quickly on necessary staff reductions.

What does it mean to the company?

In addition to the knowledge that they have done the "right thing," it can produce major overhead savings through the timely removal of excess personnel. Also, in this time of increasing regulatory activity and concern over the rights of employees, outplacement marketing is a well-timed development.

The Performance Dynamics Outplacement Marketing Program

In our role as America's leading outplacement consulting firm, we have dealt with thousands of clients from virtually every discipline and industry. A description of exactly what our own firm does for an individual is probably the easiest way for you to understand what outplacement marketing really involves. When a corporation retains us to provide our executive outplacement marketing program, the sequence of services normally provided is as follows:

1. We can have a member of our staff on hand when a termination takes place. Typically, we explain our services and help reduce trauma involved with the situation. The individual is brought to our firm for comprehensive instruction by from 4 to 8 members of our executive staff. All of the most sophisticated job hunting techniques and our own system of personal marketing are covered. A wealth of up-to-date information on the job markets is also provided.

2. After gathering full background information about an individual, our firm then prepares a complete marketing plan to enable the person to target himself against the right career fields and industries, and to generate significant interview activity on a planned schedule. After the marketing plan has been presented in private consultation, a detailed written summary report is also supplied.

3. Personal advice is then offered to help the individual develop and project the proper image. This includes suggestions relative to personal dress and grooming, as well as development of a complete interviewing and negotiating plan for the individual to pursue. At the same time, interviewing skills are normally refined through practice sessions in our color television studios.

4. Our firm then prepares all necessary resumes and letters for the individual. This can include multiple resumes in support of different job campaign objectives, as well as up to 10 job search letters for use in contacting different types of individuals.

Needless to say our objective is to produce outstanding materials of commanding distinction . . . creative work which captures the best possible expression of each person's capabilities. All paper selection, typesetting and resume printing needs are also taken care of for the individual.

5. An affiliate of ours, specializing in job market research, then provides full research assistance. This includes use of a computer for complete selection of employers, executive search firms and high-level employment agencies for contact. Additionally, the entire published job market in the U.S., England and Canada is surveyed on a daily basis, and every outplacement candidate is apprised of all suitable openings that come on the market.

6. Lastly, a weekly newsletter highlighting growth opportunities is supplied. With the campaign ready for launch, we then market the individual to carefully selected organizations throughout the world. As the candidate goes through his job campaign, our consultants are available to work with the individual on every phase of the job search until a new position has been successfully negotiated.

Obviously, if you happen to find yourself in a position where you are being terminated, you would be wise to request outplacement assistance. In fact, today, talented people who find themselves blocked from growth in an organization, are better off sitting down with their employer and negotiating outplacement on a mutually acceptable basis.

While there is no outplacement firm that can guarantee your success, our own outplacement assignments over the last 3 years have resulted in more than 85% of all individuals winning new positions at better levels of responsibility or compensation. The average person also increased his income by 25%, while the percentage who changed careers or industries exceeded 33%.

CHAPTER 13

Maintaining Secrecy / The Handling of References / Application Forms

Unfortunately for job hunters, secrecy during a job campaign can never be assured. However, I can suggest certain unconventional approaches which will allow you to explore select opportunities with a minimum of risk.

One possibility you could consider would be to make use of a post office box number as your address. For example, for a period of three months you could get a box number at a post office that is not in your own community. You should be able to get one at a post office convenient enough for you to check a few times a week.

You would then be free to send your resume (less your name) and unsigned letters in answer to blind advertisements. In these cases, I suggest you indicate the delicate nature of your present position necessitates anonymity until you know who they are, or can establish a mutual interest in confidence.

If you are looking for a position in your industry, this anonymous approach can be surprisingly effective. You don't have to tell too much about yourself and can more easily avoid highlighting any liabilities in your background.

The fact that you have specialized knowledge of someone's business is usually enough to pique their interest. I have always felt that its success is also somewhat related to its mystery appeal. Since it is rarely used, the individual on the receiving end may grant an interview simply because of curiosity factors.

Third Party Approach

The most common way to protect your identity involves making use of a third party. Here I refer to your using a friend's assistance in answering advertisements, sending direct mail letters, and so forth. This third party approach can be troublesome and less efficient in terms of time. On the other hand, boastful statements are in much better taste when they come from someone else.

This method can work for people seeking from $50,000 to $150,000. In fact, I personally know of a number of top executives who successfully marketed themselves with this approach. However, to make it work you must execute this type of campaign with tact and sophistication, and you need a close and talented associate to help you.

Third Party Approach —
With You as the Third Party

A less desirable alternative would involve use of a bogus name. You could answer all ads with a letter, and contact companies where you state that you know of a person and are acting on his behalf. You would state your own qualities and then divulge that you were the applicant when you receive a call or letter indicating interest. This should be done only as a last resort.

If you consider using any of the above approaches and want to use a resume rather than just a letter, you will obviously require a special resume. To best protect your anonymity, it should be a simple typewritten resume which *does not* contain the names of any of your employers or schools, or your name and address.

As previously indicated, there is no technique which can eliminate all risk. However, we have known people who circulated up to 1,500 resumes under the cover of a box number, or with third party assistance, and who achieved their goals.

The Handling of References

It is generally unwise to give the names of references until you are quite certain a job offer will be extended. For one thing, if you give out your references too frequently, you may find that these people become annoyed. Then when you really need them you might not end up with as strong an endorsement.

If you are not sure of your references or about your past employer's opinion of you, you should have them checked in advance of your campaign. On many occasions, people have received lukewarm references which were contrary to their expectations.

If you do have some doubts, you could have a friend at another company make a phone call to the reference in question. This could be done in the guise of an employer who is considering hiring you. As an alternative, you could do the same thing by letter.

The content of this type of letter would say that you had applied for a position with that company, and that your application was receiving serious attention. Your friend could then state that since you had listed their name, a comment on your quality of work, character, dates of employment and earnings would be appreciated.

If you receive either no reply or a less-than-adequate response, you should then go to that reference and indicate that he cost you an excellent opportunity. You will have to do this in good taste but you should be firm and show your disappointment. Chances are that it would never happen again, since giving you a poor reference would not be worth the legal trouble an individual might cause for himself.

If the above action doesn't work out, be sure to give advance notice to your potential employer of the differences existing between you and the reference in question.

The whole area of cross-checking your references can be extremely delicate. Making a check on yourself can completely backfire if you handle it the wrong way. I know of one instance where a gentleman quit an organization, but was concerned about the reference he would receive. He decided to do his own check through a post office box number which was one hundred miles away.

He invented a bogus organization, gave it the box number address and had stationery printed. He subsequently sent a letter to the personnel executive explaining that he was an applicant for a job and requested a reference on himself. He signed the letter with an alias name.

Approximately five days later, the job applicant received a letter at the box number. Unfortunately, it was personally addressed to him, rather than to his alias. The letter read, *"Dear John, I am astonished that you would stoop so low that you would try and perpetrate something like this."* The letter was signed by the personnel executive of his former employer.

It was at this stage that the job applicant came to our firm for advice! Needless to say, he was shocked at having been discovered and worried about losing his reference forever. It turned out to be only the beginning of his problems, since he had also sent the same letter to other executives at the same organization.

When this gentleman's problem was unraveled, it turned out that he underestimated the executive with whom he was dealing. The latter had felt the letter was a bogus one because of the box number and the absence of a phone number. He then wrote his reply, drove the hundred miles and handed the envelope to a postal employee. He indicated that he had forgotten the person's box number and name of his firm. In essence, he tricked the post office into revealing that the job applicant was the user of the box. The moral of this case is obvious. If you check your references, make sure you do the job well.

Outstanding references can be a tremendous help to almost any person. You should try to cultivate references from individuals with impressive titles. Listing references which include senators, congressmen, generals, chief executives, publishers or other people in the public limelight will impress almost anyone. If you have these kinds of references, be sure to make use of them.

The Handling of Application Forms

Application forms provide job hunters with a totally unique source of frustration. Completing them can be immensely time consuming. Furthermore, the forms always manage to highlight liabilities and allow minimum room for expression of achievements.

As a general rule, you should try to make sure that an interesting position is available before you complete them. An even better policy is to try to avoid them entirely.

Of course, if you are answering ads or sending letters to firms, you will almost certainly receive correspondence including application forms. In many cases you will have to complete them prior to getting an interview. Some pointers on handling them are listed below:

1. When filling out applications, always type or print neatly, and keep erasures to a minimum. Never fill them out in a hurry, and always fill them out at home. If someone requests that you complete one in an office lobby prior to an interview, simply indicate that you would rather fill it out at your own convenience.

2. If the salary objective is requested on a given form, you should generally leave it blank. It is virtually impossible to guess accurately about how much a position is worth, and stating your objective can only limit your ability to negotiate.

3. You should generally avoid filling in references until you are sure a mutual interest exists.

4. When you complete your occupation history, be sure to expand on the accomplishments and duties section by referring them to your resume.

5. Make sure that you reflect an active personality on questions concerning hobbies. A good mixture of sports, civic affairs and social interests is usually satisfactory.

6. Questions along the line of "Have you been arrested or denied credit within the last five years?" — invite the obvious response! It is illegal for an employer to ask these questions under the Equal Employment Opportunity Law!

7. If an application requests college grades, and you happen to be near the bottom of your class, be sure to emphasize part-time jobs and other activities while in college.

8. When you return your application, attach a well-written cover letter which clearly restates your desire to explore the particular opportunity.

There are some employers in the country who make use of "handwriting analysis" as a screening procedure. Your tip-off to this will be when you see a request in the application form that asks you to write 10 to 15 lines in "longhand." They usually supply an unlined blank area and want you to write with a regular ball point pen.

The theory behind "graphology" is that brain impulses subconsciously manifest themselves in handwriting. I do not pretend to be a graphologist, and am not certain about the validity of this practice as a recruiting tool. Nevertheless, there are a few books on the subject and one of my associates offered me the following generalities:

1. *Writing which is slanted to the left (by righties)* may indicate an impersonal and cold nature, or a perfectionist.

2. *Inconsistent spacing between words or letters* may indicate a disorganized thinker, someone who cannot plan.

3. *Very wide spacing* may indicate a lack of ambition, someone who won't work very hard.

4. *Wavelike lines* may indicate a warm, friendly and trustworthy nature.

5. *Large, aggressive and curved arches* may indicate a very outgoing, perhaps extroverted, personality.

6. *Failure to close slopes of looped letters* (e.g. o's, a's and g's) may indicate someone who is not trustworthy or not able to respect confidentialities.

7. *Retracing of letters* may indicate that the writer may be capable of thievery.

8. *Capital letters slanted to the left,* while the rest of the work goes to the right, may indicate very strong guilt feelings.

Regardless of the above, I have yet to hear of a single person who has been turned down for a job simply because of handwriting.

CHAPTER 14

Communications Strategy and SODAR

Early in our consulting experience, it became apparent that many of our clients needed to focus on more than just generating interviews. Certainly, a good marketing plan, the right contacts, and superior written materials could produce attractive interview opportunities.

However, having gained initial interest, we found that talented people would still lose out on opportunities which they should have won. What they lacked was a way for effectively describing strengths and achievements.

After coaching thousands to improve their skills in this area, we analyzed our methods and found that our help could be classified within three basic areas. They were: (1) Development of a Communications Strategy, (2) Development of personally descriptive "Key Words and Concepts," and (3) Making use of a communications technique called SODAR.

Development of a Communications Strategy

The role of a communications strategy can probably best be appreciated by comparing it to the "platform" of a candidate for the Presidency of the United States. The "platform" anticipates questions on major issues by formulating carefully thought-out position statements to guide the candidate's answers. This enables a person to answer difficult questions with confidence . . . while making sure that important points are always put across.

Just like the political candidate, you can be perceived as more informed, intelligent, and positive than the next person . . . if you have taken the time to formulate your communications strategy.

To do this, you must think through your assets, liabilities, and goals, and then arrive at a general formula which will guide your communications about yourself. The strategy itself must be geared to maximizing your strong points and minimizing any liabilities.

Naturally, a communications strategy will vary for each individual. For some it will be to your advantage to stress the promotions you've received and the titles you have held. For others, who may not have a clear history of growth, it may prove most helpful to emphasize the substance of what you have achieved. For still another, you might focus on the many functions in which you have some expertise.

Remember, employers will tend to evaluate job candidates on the basis of their experience, knowledge and achievement. Be sure to emphasize, with proper balance, all three. Don't rely on experience alone to do all the selling for you.

If you have a notable weakness, you may be able to offset it by citing a number of closely related strengths. Or, it may be appropriate for you to group certain jobs in your discussions, or to emphasize a past position rather than your present one.

Regardless, it will pay you to take the time to identify every strength, anticipate every problem, and formulate a platform to guide your responses to any discussion you might encounter. When you know precisely what you have to offer, and how you want to communicate yourself, you can come across with superior effectiveness in all interviews.

Development of Personally Descriptive Key Words and Concepts

What sets you apart from those who are competing with you? Most people, when faced with the need to sell themselves, will fall into one of two pitfalls.

They may overstate their qualifications ("There isn't any job I can't handle"). Or, they may simply begin to talk about their past duties. Since many other applicants are likely to have the same duties, this latter direction can make you appear quite average.

You can avoid these common errors if you take the time to build a vocabulary of key words and concepts which apply particularly to you. Obviously, this must be done in advance of your interviews.

As an exercise, I suggest you review your past experience and begin to make a list of key words and short phrases which describe your individual accomplishments and the strengths you used to attain them.

For instance, you might have "established harmony where conflict previously existed," or you may have "operated efficiently under heavy pressure." Perhaps you are "an excellent motivator," or you may have "built a highly effective team." If you are young and are short on experience, you may be long on personal characteristics. One of your strengths may be that you are "a good listener" or "someone who can work easily with people at virtually any level."

A key word or concept can describe a personal characteristic not related to a specific achievement, or it might refer to a particular action or experience.

Most people with five or more years of work experience can make a list of at least 20 key words and concepts. Used appropriately in an interview situation, they can build a very precise word picture of your strengths and capabilities. They can conceptually set you apart from competition and accurately convey the unique advantages you have to offer.

Making Use of the SODAR Technique

The use of key words and concepts is fine as far as it goes. The problem is that for most people it is difficult to deal purely in concepts. They may understand them, but will often forget them in minutes. A concept without an example is not memorable.

A concept without an example may also lack credibility. If, for instance, you were to make the claim that you are someone who can "implement major changes," but you cannot cite an example, then your claim will appear shallow.

In order to assure that your points are both memorable and credible, you can use a method we invented called our SODAR technique. SODAR represents a particular way of describing your past experience. It is an acronym which stands for . . . Situation . . . Opportunities . . . Duties . . . Actions . . . Results.

Here's how you can use it. Rather than speaking of a job you held in terms of your duties, you should first describe the SITUATION when you began employment. This enables you to provide some interesting background information, e.g., what had been taking place when you arrived.

Then you should integrate into your discussion information about the OPPORTUNITIES which the job seemed to present to you, the group you were part of, and the firm.

Subsequently, you should describe your DUTIES. However, more importantly, your emphasis should quickly move to those ACTIONS taken by you and other members of your team, and what RESULTS occurred because of your efforts.

In essence, using SODAR means "telling the whole story, rather than describing routine job duties." As far as your listeners are concerned, a well-told story will generate more genuine interest and impact than a listing of responsibilities. Furthermore, it will help people remember you ahead of others, because people remember stories, while they tend to forget duties or concepts.

(To illustrate a specific concept with a shorter example, you may wish to consider a shorthand version of the SODAR, namely S-A-R., i.e., Situation-Actions-Results. You will find the abbreviated SODAR format to also be a very handy tool for creating short but action-oriented stories.)

In preparing yourself, I suggest that for every concept you want to use, you construct a SODAR story to support it. Try to describe the situation in a manner which sets up the challenge you faced. Tell what actions you took. And then describe the results in quantifiable terms.

An important point: In developing your S-A-R examples, try to avoid the word "we" whenever possible as it dilutes the strength of your personal contribution. You are selling your own accomplishments, personal characteristics and experience — so don't hesitate to use the pronoun "I." The prospective employer is buying "you" — not the team!

To become really good at emphasizing your strong points, you must work on your SODAR stories. One way to do this is to dictate them into a recorder, and listen to how you come across. Keep the stories short and try not to fill them with extraneous detail. With some practice, you will find that during your interviews they flow quite naturally as a regular part of the conversation.

Many clients have told us that it was their use of carefully rehearsed SODAR stories which most impressed an interviewer and won job offers for them. This is hardly unexpected. Anyone who has listened to a speech or a sales presentation knows how much more interesting it can be if the speaker uses short stories to demonstrate a point. Remember this as you build your SODAR stories.

CHAPTER 15

The Handling of Psychological Tests for Employment Screening Purposes

In the 1960's and early 1970's, both psychological and aptitude testing were really in vogue. Since then the use of testing in personnel selection has declined. Only at junior levels are short aptitude tests still commonly used.

The reasons behind the decline in testing are quite simple. The major factor involves the Equal Employment Opportunity legislation. Because of these laws, testing has been under close scrutiny from special interest groups.

Another contributing factor concerns the validity of most tests. Their accuracy at predicting executive success has rarely been established in concrete form.

A third factor is that organizations have found that many candidates prefer not to submit to testing.

While faking a professional test battery is not easy, the situation has grown even more complicated because experienced test-takers can finesse certain tests. In short, they are able to project the image they desire.

During your job search you will still encounter firms which request that you take tests. At the executive level, unless you enjoy it and can turn this to an advantage, you shouldn't be willing to take them. Tests are simply a screening out device. You will still need to possess all the qualities necessary for any other employment position.

The easiest way to decline taking a test is to indicate that at this stage in your career, you prefer to stand on your record of accomplishments. You can also add that you would be happy to supply business or personal references if your representation of yourself is questioned.

There are some people who suggest that any refusal to take tests is bad strategy. They will tell you that your unwillingness can only cause an employer to wonder about the other things you will refuse to do.

The fact is that test taking should be a two-way street. It is just as important for you to know more about your direct superior as it is for your employer to know more about you. I sincerely doubt, however, that any employer would offer to share with you the results of tests taken by your potential boss!

If you find you simply cannot avoid taking some tests, I suggest you approach them with care. You may be at quite a disadvantage. This is because the more widely used tests have fallen into the hands of a great number of people.

If you have some weak areas, you risk rejection because of the superior performance of those who have experience with the tests. Even if you have excellent aptitude and are psychologically well-balanced, it is likely that your best effort *will only be performance at a level achieved by many other applicants.*

There are some excellent books written on all phases and types of testing. The best ones are of the textbook variety and are used in teaching at the university level.

Although it is quite old, *The Organization Man* by William Whyte contains some provocative discussions as well as advice to test-takers. Another interesting book is *The Brain Watchers* by Martin Gross. It is an exposé type of book in which the testing industry is indicted. Nevertheless, it does have some cogent material on how to score well.

If you really want to learn more about testing, as well as more about yourself, I suggest that you give some consideration to the test services available at your nearest university. You can usually arrange to take any type of test through the psychology departments of these institutions.

Executives would do better with one of the four or five nationwide firms who specialize in testing for industry. This is because the university testers may lack the business test standards, the experience in business, and the understanding of what specific management jobs may or may not require.

Some Brief Preparation for Psychological Tests

The object of almost all psychological tests is to enable a firm to obtain a description of your strengths and weaknesses. However, during all interviews and tests, your object is to project the image which will assist you in getting job offers. Obviously, these two objectives will almost always be in direct conflict.

There is presently a wide range of different tests in use. The techniques employed can vary from long discussions with a psychologist, to tests where you view a series of ink-blots and describe what you see.

The most common tests, however, are of the written variety. These tests normally ask you questions about what you think of your parents, friends, superiors, and yourself. They will generally ask you about your perceptions of the influence which these people have exercised on you. They also probe for your opinion on how others view your personality.

From your point of view, the most difficult thing about these tests will relate to your ability to project a consistent image. If you are unable to do this, the firm will assume that you either lack intelligence or were not cooperating on their tests.

Achieving consistency is difficult because almost all tests will ask similar questions (with changed phrasing) in different parts of the same test. They are usually referred to as built-in lie detectors, and can be difficult to finesse when you are subjected to a lengthy test battery.

In order to provide you with general guidance as well as specific assistance regarding this consistency problem, I think you should participate in a short exercise.

You will find below a list of 183 words. These words comprise almost all of the general personality and ability traits commonly measured by any type of psychological test. The words themselves actually form the basic vocabulary used in the profile report which would be the end result of many tests. In fact, this list is complete enough to permit a profile description of you or any individual you know.

Test Instructions

Assume that an employer instructed you as follows:

In three minutes, please go through the list of words and check those positive and negative factors which most consistently apply to you.

You can check any number of positive factors that apply, but you must check a minimum of 10 negative ones.

Generally positive

active	detailed	honest	poised
adaptable	determined	imaginative	positive
aggressive	dignified	independent	practical
alert	diplomatic	individualist	productive
ambitious	discerning	inspiring	proud
analytical	disciplined	intellectual	purposeful
argumentative	discreet	intuitive	realistic
artistic	discriminating	just	reliable
astute	economical	keen	resourceful
attentive	efficient	kind	respected
broad-minded	eloquent	logical	self-reliant
composed	energetic	loyal	sense-of-humor
congenial	enterprising	methodical	shrewd
conscientious	enthusiastic	modest	sincere
considerate	esteemed	objective	sociable
consistent	exacting	observant	sophisticated
constructive	extroverted	opinionated	sympathetic
contemplative	fair	optimistic	systematic
courageous	forceful	orderly	tactful
courteous	forward-thinking	outspoken	talented
creative	frank	patient	thoughtful
cultured	friendly	perceptive	tolerant
daring	generous	perfectionist	truthful
democratic	genuine	personable	visionary
dependable	good-natured	philosophical	

Generally negative

abrupt	domineering	introverted	self-conscious
agitator	easily depressed	jealous	selfish
agnostic	eccentric	lavish	sensitive
anti-social	egotistical	lethargic	sentimental
arrogant	embittered	mean	shallow
avaricious	emotional	mutinous	simple
awkward	excitable	naive	skeptic
bizarre	fabricator	negligent	stubborn
bogus	fastidious	obstinate	submissive
bungler	forgetful	paltry	superficial
capricious	fragile	pessimistic	suspicious
clumsy	impractical	pompous	temperamental
complacent	impulsive	possessive	trivial
conceited	inconsiderate	pretentious	two-faced
conventional	inconsistent	rash	uncertain
corrupt	incorrigible	repugnant	unobservant
covetous	indifferent	reserved	unreliable
crafty	inhibited	restless	unscrupulous
deceitful	irritable	sarcastic	unsophisticated
despondent	insubordinate	secretive	vacillating
discourteous	intolerable	self-centered	vicious

Now that you have checked these words, be totally honest with yourself in admitting how well you would come out if you were confronted as follows:

Situation A — The interviewer asks you to describe to him verbally, the reasons prompting your selection of each word, and to support that selection with actual examples of accomplishments. You must also state the names of other individuals in the situations you describe (e.g., your employer, a business associate, your father, etc.).

Situation B — The interviewer takes your completed list, and then invites you back for more interviewing in one week. At that time, he gives you the same list, but with the words intermingled, and asks you to again complete the test.

Situation C — The interviewer takes your completed list and informs you that instead of subjecting applicants to lengthy tests, their policy is to send the same list to your references and former supervisors. These people would be asked to describe you by checking the words under the same ground rules. The interviewer says they seek to effect a simple confirmation of your self-image.

The Lessons From This Exercise

The first point is that on any given test you are at the mercy of the methodology and the individual doing the interpretation. In the best of situations, there is much to be desired in terms of true objectivity.

The forced-choice test, which is most common, is particularly difficult because you frequently receive inadequate instructions. When you looked at the test words you probably thought that "this describes me sometimes, in some settings, but not in others." Or perhaps you thought that a great many of the words applied to you on different occasions, but that there were variations in degree. These frustrations are exactly what you will encounter when you try to be forthright on tests.

The second point to be observed is that many tests are evaluated as much by what you fail to check, as by what you do check. Furthermore, they are usually full of synonyms. You might find it worthwhile to go back and look at the positive qualities which you omitted. You should consider what they might reveal to someone about positive characteristics *which you don't believe you possess.*

Insofar as synonyms are concerned, there are many words on the tests which have almost identical meaning. Many people who administer tests assume that if you check one word you should also check others with the same meaning (e.g., reliable and dependable). Any failure to do so subsequently reflects on either your honesty or intelligence.

The third point of this exercise is that it presents you with the problem of how good an image to project. If you presented too perfect an image, the people conducting the test may not believe you. More significantly, they may catch you in your fabrication by presenting you with a situation similar to examples A and C.

On the other hand, you obviously don't want to project too many weaknesses. If you did this, you might fail to meet the criteria established for the job.

The best approach to both of these questions is to project a normal, less-than-perfect image. Everyone has faults and a person without weaknesses just doesn't exist.

However, you should be sure to lean to the positive qualities and project the negative which would be least likely to affect your ability to do any given job. For example, being "reserved" may not be a negative at all. The same holds true for "skeptic," "sensitive," "sentimental," etc.

Some of the words on the negative list may actually be desirable in a specific situation. Likewise, some of the words listed as positive factors could be considered undesirable traits.

Some negatives are also much worse than others. For example, being "belligerent" may certainly be unattractive. However, it is probably far better than being "corrupt" or "deceitful." What you will need to project will depend upon your occupation and your estimation of what traits the employer is likely to associate with projected success.

By the way, if you can honestly say that none of the assumed test situations created any feeling of panic, then you are probably a master at test-taking who has nothing to worry about. However, if you reacted to the exercise as most people do, there are some wise lessons to be learned.

Reference situation A — If you really expect to face the first situation, as you might in a session with a psychologist, you could be prepared. The first thing you should do is to go over the words on the list. They can help to refresh your knowledge of yourself, and help you formulate the image you want to project. If you understand yourself and know the image you want to convey, you will have a much easier time understanding the object of any question in any test situation. Almost any question you will face will have as its object the identification of one of the traits on the list.

Reference situation B — If you were faced with the second situation you would probably have a hard time maintaining your consistency. This would be particularly true if you had not done some serious thinking about the image you desire to project. You can beat this type of situation by having a keen awareness of synonyms and antonyms, and by sticking firmly to your pattern of answering questions.

Reference situation C — If an employer presented you with the third situation, either forget about the job, or don't let it worry you at all. While employers do look for consistency in any reference check, the lack of it is no condemnation of any person. In fact, if you really were an adaptable individual, you would probably be wise to project different attributes in different social and business situations.

I believe you will find it worthwhile to do some thinking about the words on the test exercise. In order to facilitate this, the list below restates the words in homogeneous groups. I also suggest that you refer to these words when writing your resume. Many people have found them to be a stimulating source of ideas.

Family Groupings of Words With Some Homogeneity

Generally positive

courteous	composed	realistic	optimistic
sociable	poised	practical	positive
personable	sophisticated	economical	forward-thinker
friendly	cultured	efficient	visionary
congenial			individual
good-natured	consistent	proud	independent
	orderly	eloquent	self-reliant
thoughtful	methodical	dignified	enterprising
contemplative	systematic	esteemed	
considerate	detailed	inspiring	observant
kind	perfectionist		attentive
sympathetic		active	alert
generous	reliable	energetic	
	dependable	enthusiastic	logical
tolerant	loyal		analytical
patient	honest	aggressive	
	truthful	ambitious	intuitive
genuine		forceful	perceptive
sincere	disciplined	exacting	discerning
conscientious	determined		astute
fair	purposeful	outspoken	keen
just	constructive	argumentative	shrewd
democratic	productive	opinionated	
broad-minded		extroverted	intellectual
objective			philosophical
	creative	talented	
	imaginative		tactful
daring	resourceful	sense-of-humor	discreet
courageous	adaptable		diplomatic
		artistic	modest

Generally negative

abrupt
awkward
clumsy
bungler
ineffectual

capricious
forgetful
negligent
unobservant
unreliable

complacent
lethargic
indifferent

restless
inconsistent
irritable

emotional
temperamental
excitable
impulsive
rash

squeamish
fastidious

bizarre
eccentric

agitator
insubordinate
mutinous

secretive
fabricator
crafty
deceitful

corrupt
two-faced
incorrigible
unscrupulous

jealous
possessive
covetous
avaricious

trivial
paltry
selfish

skeptic
agnostic

fragile
reserved

inhibited
self-conscious
sensitive
introverted
submissive

vacillating
uncertain

discourteous
inconsiderate
sarcastic
embittered
vicious
mean

despondent
easily depressed
pessimistic

conventional
simple
shallow

sentimental

anti-social
belligerent
repugnant
intolerable
domineering

self-centered
conceited

egotistical
pretentious
arrogant
pompous

stubborn
obstinate
narrow-minded
impractical

naive
unsophisticated

superficial
bogus

extravagant
lavish

CHAPTER 16

The Interview

Everything you do in a job campaign will be wasted if you don't convert interviews into job offers. In order to make effective use of our system, it is important that you review this chapter very carefully.

Our philosophy requires that you be *informed* about potential employers; that you *plan to control your interviews;* and that you *tailor your communications and the image* you project to what each firm is seeking.

Be Informed About the Firms You Visit

Before you go to an interview, you should always try to learn as much as possible about each company. This means being familiar with a firm's products, markets, number of employees, current stock quotation, growth record, recent sales' profits and problems.

If you understand their concerns in relation to the job you seek, then you will be in a better position to demonstrate how you can be of value.

The principal sources for information on public companies are brokerage house reports, company annual reports, D & B reports, *Fortune* magazine's directory, Moody's manuals, and special yearly issues of trade magazines.

Advertising Age and *Forbes* are two media which publish special annual information on leading corporations. *Predicasts F&S Index* can also give you references to articles on specific firms. It covers over 750 leading business and trade magazines, and is available in most large libraries.

The Wall Street Journal and *The New York Times* indexes are sources for articles highlighting recent developments in specific companies. If you are being interviewed by a prominent executive, his background may appear in *"Who's Who."* Some research here may help you identify in advance some things you have in common.

The Interview . . .
Things You Should Do

I strongly believe that applicants at all levels should be very well prepared, and that with preparation and the right technique, they can control the direction and pace of any interview. In most interviewing situations, some of the obvious but critical things you should do are as follows:

Dress well

A blue suit is still the best compromise in view of all the types of people you will meet. Worn suits, frayed shirts, and shoes with holes in them won't help you. The same holds true for women who wear heavy makeup and mod clothing.

Bow ties, shaded glasses, and dress which is out of the ordinary are becoming somewhat more acceptable. Solid blue or white shirts are still your best bet. Most of all, wear clothes that fit. Also, don't forget the obvious; use a mouthwash and deodorant, and go easy on the aftershave or perfume.

In general, most people do best by dressing conservatively and trying to appear as relaxed, neatly groomed and successful as possible. Remember, your clothes talk for you before you open your mouth. In short, make sure you look and act like a winner.

Gain control

In order to take control of an interview, you must avert the superior-to-subordinate relationship that carries through most interviewing situations. You'll need to be socially gregarious and aggressive . . . without being obnoxious. You'll also want to appear learned, charming and diplomatic.

You can avoid intimidation and can satisfactorily establish the tempo of most interviews by assuming the role of the one who initially asks the questions.

We recommend that when people meet an interviewer, they give a firm and enthusiastic handshake, and then initiate the discussion. One way to do this, for example, would be to start by complimenting a person on something in his office, and subsequently raising a question about the object on which you have commented.

Speak clearly

When you are asked questions you should be brief but positive. Watch your speech, speak slowly, articulate as clearly as possible and avoid "and . . . ah's" or other verbal slips.

Use a soft sell

Always underplay your need for a new job, and always use a soft-sell approach. You'll be on your way to an offer when the firm starts recruiting you!

Be truthful

You should do your best to tell the truth, and be as forthright and consistent as possible. If your background includes mental illness, homosexuality, bankruptcy, alcoholism or a prison term . . . don't volunteer the information.

However, if you are asked, tell the truth without being defensive or feeling abnormal. If these things apply, you will need to develop your own approaches for handling them in a delicate manner.

Calm your nerves

If you are high-strung or inclined to nervousness, consider taking a mild tranquilizer before an interview. Better yet, be sure to exercise every day and get 8 hours sleep. This age-old prescription still works wonders for people who need to control their nerves.

Be professional
Maintain your professionalism at all times. If your dignity is abused, then close out the interview and go on to better things.

Image yourself
At all times you should project ambition, enthusiasm, and confidence. However, you will need to control your ambition in line with your estimation of each situation. Before you go to an interview, you should plan on projecting an image of yourself which is tailored to the requirements of the specific position.

In addition to the general qualities related to your occupational field, you would usually be wise to convey three very important image qualities: sincerity, a dedication to achievement, and a high-energy level.

Emphasize the most important things
Wherever possible you should gear your comments to potential contributions relative to sales, profits, cost reduction, innovations or growth.

Be ready for the periods of silence
When there is a period of silence, you should have questions you are prepared to raise about the field or industry, for which you have answers. The object in doing this is to create an opportunity which will enable you to demonstrate your knowledge and relate your past experiences which are relevant to the solution of their problems.

Protect your present employer
Always protect the confidence of your present employer and do not be overly critical of your existing situation. Any breach in this area will quickly close out your opportunity. This is because the potential employers will assume that someday you'll do the same thing to them.

Use flattery

Always be prepared to say something which will indicate admiration for certain achievements of the organization or its top management. In the interview situation, a brief amount of flattery will help. Overdo it, and it will work against you.

Project good health

If you are asked, you should state that your health is excellent.

Be a good listener

Make sure that you are a good listener, extremely observant, and that you learn something about your interviewer's interests and background. You may wish to use this information in your letter which will follow up the interview. Being a good listener also means that you'll be able to ask good questions.

Question the interviewer

One of the easiest ways to impress people is to ask intelligent and penetrating questions about the firm and the position. Areas for possible exploration include the following:

— Find out what happened to the last person in the job, and if possible get his name.

— Identify how many people have had the same position and where they have gone. The tip-off is heavy turnover.

— Determine the company's method for handling budgets and purchase orders. If they make it difficult for people to get paper clips, chances are they won't delegate much authority in other areas. In order for you to succeed, you obviously need the opportunity to fail.

— Learn about the chief of the company. Many companies directly reflect the personality of the top man, and their presidents may like to promote people like themselves.

— Ask about the organization's negative factors. Find out how long the interviewer has been there and see what he says about his own experience.

— Find out if they hire friends and relatives. Are they qualified? If not, nepotism can be a real monster!

— When the interviewer has briefly covered a subject of interest you should never hesitate asking him to further expand, define or describe.

— If a situation begins to stall, you can always raise questions about any subject by merely asking who? what? when? where? why? and how?

The Interview . . .
Things You Should Avoid

Some advice relative to things you should avoid doing in any interview include the following:

Avoid application forms

Never fill out applications in waiting rooms. See the person first; then if you are interested, you can take your time and fill out the form very carefully at home.

Don't be interviewed by substitutes

Don't be interviewed by more junior substitutes, or allow yourself to be subjected to hasty interviews over the phone. Also, don't submit to an inquisition or tripartite interview.

Don't be early

Try to avoid arriving too early for an interview. This makes people seem overanxious and too available. Being on time is the answer.

Don't be kept waiting

If you are kept waiting for 25 minutes, then ask for another appointment and excuse yourself. Also, don't fumble with a heavy coat or packages. Have them put in a closet for you.

Keep your liabilities to yourself

When they are pinpointed, never apologize for any of your liabilities.

Don't flaunt your resume

Don't volunteer your resume until it is requested.

Avoid hard liquor at lunch

At lunch don't select sloppy or hard-to-manage foods. Take your cue on drinks from the interviewer, and stay with lighter drinks such as wine. Avoid smoking unless the interviewer lights up first.

Never be a threat

Be careful about posing a threat to your prospective boss's position. People will say that they want to hire people who are better than themselves — but most of the time they don't mean it!

Don't act curious or bored

Never read the mail on your interviewer's desk, nervously drum your fingers, look at your watch, or exhibit other signs of boredom.

Don't discuss controversial subjects

You should generally avoid discussions on race, religion, or politics. They can only invite trouble.

Don't promise miracles

Also, despite projecting confidence, you should never imply you can do everything or that you are a miracle worker. People won't believe you!

Don't be a braggart or name-dropper

Don't be a "yes-man"; don't interrupt; don't lose your temper; and when you are selling yourself, don't do it in a way that makes you a braggart. Also, don't name-drop unless you can be extremely smooth about it. Name-dropping usually backfires.

Keep your references to yourself

In general, try to avoid naming your references until the very end. If you give your references out too often you'll find they will be less effective when you need them.

Don't be pressured

Don't permit yourself to get flustered by the presence of unusual decor, strange lighting, uncomfortable chairs, an interviewer's finger tapping, or some phone interruptions.

Never be pressured into accepting a permanent job at a lower level than you seek. Inside of one month you may regret it!

Don't offer samples of your work

Never bring unsolicited samples of your work or give out confidential information about your past employer.

Note: Certain occupational areas may require exception to this. For example, if you happen to be a copywriter or an art director, you would be wise to maintain an impressive portfolio of your work, and use it as evidence of your accomplishments.

Don't let interviews drag

Don't let an interview carry on too long. You should be able to sense when a discussion has peaked, and unless an offer may be forthcoming, you should diplomatically lead to an end of the meeting. Also, don't linger after the interview is finished.

After Every Interview —
Follow Up With a Letter

The practice of following up every interview with a letter will probably be your single most critical job search technique. The use of such a letter is basic to our system of changing jobs, and *will positively bring results which you otherwise would not achieve.*

Follow-up letters give you a chance to reinforce your image after an interviewer has probably been exposed to other attractive candidates. I am not speaking of standard "thank you" letters. I'm referring to a letter which restates your prime assets and accomplishments, along with what you can do for a firm.

The style of the follow-up letters should be warm and friendly, but you may find it useful to touch upon major subjects which you discussed, and if possible, use names and language which reflect the company environment.

If your follow-up letter does not bring a reply, you must then follow up with a telephone call in which you display continued enthusiasm. Very few job candidates make use of the follow-up, and it is definitely the *most neglected* technique in job changing.

In a survey of 2,000 people, we once found that most middle managers were able to convert less than 1 out of every 10 interviews into a job offer. If you make tasteful use of regular follow-up, in connection with our approach to interviewing, you will take a big step toward insuring your success.

Prepare Thoroughly for Interview Questions

Though every interview (and interviewer) is different, there are positive steps you can take to develop skills which will keep you at your best in almost all interviews.

On the following pages, I have listed the most commonly asked interview questions. I suggest you think about your possible answers to each of these questions in advance. *This is a very critical point.* Many people develop their abilities for getting interviews, but subsequently lose out because of hesitancy and lack of poise in handling these very questions.

Some interviewers will fire these very same questions at you in rapid succession. They can be difficult to answer and will reflect on your knowledge, ability to think quickly and your confidence.

They frequently form the basis of what is commonly known as a "stress interview." In this case they are combined with other pressures such as an uncomfortable office and an interviewer's intentionally forceful personality.

Remember that above all, in order to develop finesse in this area, you're going to need to learn from your mistakes. With experience and the right attitude, almost everyone can develop skills which will gradually enable him to master all types of interview situations.

For maximum preparedness, I recommend that you verbalize possible answers out loud. Even if you are an accomplished speaker, you will be amazed at how much you can project through such an exercise. It is really not much different from a politician preparing for an open press conference, and practice will enable you to project a knowledgeable and confident image.

What are your short-range objectives? Long range?

What do you look for in a job?

Why are you leaving? Why did your business fail?

What can you do for us that someone else cannot do?

Why should we hire you?

How good is your health?

Can you work under pressure, deadlines, etc.?

What is your philosophy of management?

Do you prefer staff or line work? Why?

What kind of salary are you worth?

What are your five biggest accomplishments in your present or last job? Your career so far?

Why didn't you do better in college?

What is your biggest strength? Weakness?

What business, character, and credit references can you give us?

How long would it take to make a contribution to our firm?

How long would you stay with us?

How do you feel about people from minority groups?

If you could start again, what would you do differently?

How do you rate yourself as a professional? As an executive?

What new goals or objectives have you established recently?

How have you changed the nature of your job?

What do you think of your boss?

What is your feeling about . . . alcoholism? . . . divorce? . . . homosexuals? . . . women in business? . . . religion? . . . abortion?

Why haven't you obtained a job so far?

What features of your previous jobs have you disliked?

Would you describe a few situations in which your work was criticized?

Would you object to working for a woman?

How would you evaluate your present firm?

Do you generally speak to people before they speak to you?

How would you describe the essence of success?

What was the last book you read? Movie you saw? Sporting event you attended? etc.

In your present position, what problems have you identified that had previously been overlooked?

What interests you most about the position we have? The least?

Don't you feel you might be better off in a different size company? Different type company?

Why aren't you earning more at your age?

Will you be out to take your boss's job?

Are you creative? — Give an example.

Are you analytical? — Give an example.

Are you a good manager? — Give an example.

Are you a leader? — Give an example.

How would you describe your own personality?

Have you helped increase sales? Profits? Reduce costs?

What do your subordinates think of you?

Have you fired people before?

Have you hired people before? What do you look for?

Why do you want to work for us?

If you had your choice of jobs and companies, where would you go?

What other types of jobs are you considering? What companies?

Why do you feel you have top management potential?

Tell us about yourself.

Obviously we cannot provide answers for you to the previous questions. Every case is certainly an individual one, and the answers which you must be prepared to give will depend on your own goals and situation.

Many interviews can develop into a psychological test of wits. One of the things which you must have is a good sound reason for wanting to leave your present job. However, it can't sound like sour grapes.

You will frequently be asked to review your greatest strengths and weaknesses. Here you should have a number of answers developed in advance. You would then use the response which best fits the situation. Remember, when you are asked for your major weakness, you've got to appear mortal! The idea is to give a weakness which from the interviewer's viewpoint isn't much of a weakness.

Some examples of answers which use this type of psychology are listed on the following page:

What is your biggest weakness?

"Well, I really don't feel I have a weakness which affects my working ability. I guess at times I have a tendency to be impatient and occasionally push people too hard to get a job done. Patience isn't my strongest virtue."

What do you think of your boss?

"He's an outstanding man. I have a great deal of respect for him and have enjoyed working with him very much."

How long would it take you to make a contribution to our firm?

"Well, I hope to be able to make a contribution in a very short time. Obviously it will take some time to get my feet wet and to get used to certain operating procedures. There are a number of things which I have accomplished before that I may be able to institute once I gain a better understanding of your organization."

How long would you stay with us?

"As I mentioned to you, I'm looking for a career opportunity. However, I'm a realist. Obviously if I don't do the job you won't want me around; and if there is no opportunity for me, it won't be the type of environment I'd enjoy."

What position do you expect to have in five years?

"That really depends on the type of job I accept and the particular company I join. In some companies I might hope to be president in that length of time; while in other firms, a job with a far lesser title may prove equally enjoyable and rewarding. I guess the answer really depends on the responsibility I'm given."

What's wrong with your present firm?

"I really don't feel there is anything wrong with the firm. I have enjoyed working there and think that they have some really top people in management. It's a good company for the long pull but I am ready to handle additional responsibility right now."

Why are you leaving your present position?

"I'm anxious to earn more money and take on added responsibility. In addition to enjoying my work, I'd like to expand my knowledge. Quite frankly, these opportunities can't exist in my present positior

Concluding Comments On Interviewing

People who are sophisticated job changers invariably become masters of the entire interviewing process. They are able to rapidly determine whether an interviewer wants someone off-beat or middle-of-the-road, and whether they want a dynamo or conservative type. Then they tailor the image they project to the employer's wants.

These people also learn to quickly sense how well an interview is going and adjust their behavior accordingly.

For example, it is generally a bad sign if the interviewer continues to accept telephone calls during the course of your discussion. If he is really interested in you, he will put an end to routine interruptions.

It is generally a good sign if the interviewer does more talking than you do; if he knows your background and has read your resume before you begin the interview; or if he really begins to speak in terms of your solving his problems.

In order to convert your interviews into job offers, you probably will have to make sure your personality mixes with a number of people. This will entail the development of some expertise at complimenting strangers in a genuine and sincere manner.

For example, if you are being interviewed by a personnel executive, you should find some way to express an interest in his field, or demonstrate your recognition of his responsibility.

In any initial interview, your primary objective is to leave a very favorable impression with the interviewer. Between your interview and your follow-up, you want him to decide to actively recruit you for the organization.

There will always be some questions for which you can't have answers. However, after a while you will find that even difficult situations will leave you relatively unruffled.

When you find yourself in a situation where the job is obviously not for you, then you should use the opportunity to gain consideration for another position. If this is not possible, then you should try to gain information concerning leads to positions in other firms.

Despite the level of job hunting skill that you possess, you will also be rejected for the majority of positions for which you are interviewed. You will be rejected because you spoke too much, too soft, or too loud for a given interviewer; or because you weren't liked; or because your salary demands were too high.

However, if you have followed my advice, *you will not be rejected* because of your appearance; because your record was weak in spots without a suitable explanation; because you lacked interest in their company; because you were not communicative enough during the interview; or because your initiative was not demonstrated by the accomplishments you reviewed.

Even in the best of situations, you are going to lose quite often. One key factor will be your ability to learn from your experience and to avoid discouragement over setbacks. If you foul up an interview, don't waste time looking back and never feel embarrassed! It's a big world and you should work at exploring other opportunities.

As a final comment on interviewing, I suggest that you clarify arrangements for any expense reimbursement before the interview. If you don't do this, you are certain to end up disappointed.

In addition, I believe that when appropriate, you need to develop a tactful means of applying pressure. Don't let companies keep you on a string too long. They may just be searching for an even better prospect. Also, there will certainly be occasions where you have been interviewed by everyone concerned, but where they simply delay extending a firm offer. In such cases, your best strategy will be to indicate that while you want very much to join them other opportunities require that you have a decision within a few days.

CHAPTER 17

Salary Negotiations and Contracts

Where the Higher Salaries Exist

The greatest number of higher salaried positions exist in the large corporations and in the major cities. Also, the higher your salary requirements, *the fewer* the jobs which will be available. Of course, some industries and companies are universally lower paying than others. You should be able to identify low-paying firms from personal contacts, or in an early stage of your interview discussions.

Compensation Systems

The salary for most jobs is usually flexible within a range that is set in advance. At the very least, an employer always has an idea of what he is willing to pay for an assignment. This is true even when a firm claims that the salary is "open."

One exception to this situation would be the case where an employer wants to hire you and is willing to create a new position in order to bring you aboard. *Here you will have your best opportunity for negotiating something attractive.*

Most compensation systems make use of a range which provides for a 50% swing. For example, a company may have a position which can pay from $30,000 to $45,000. While they may prefer to hire an individual at the lowest figure possible, a widely accepted procedure is to permit offers at any amount between the minimum (i.e. $30,000) and the mid-point (i.e. $37,500).

In general, the lower the starting salary, the higher the annual percentage increase for which a person is eligible.

As an alternative, some companies follow a policy which states that the lower a person's salary (within the range), the more frequent the salary review. For example, if an individual is between the minimum and the mid-point, he may be eligible for an annual review. However, if he is between the mid-point and the maximum, he is only eligible for a review on an 18-month basis.

Regardless of your talents, many prospective employers will evaluate your potential worth to them in terms of your present earnings.

For example, if you were earning $22,000, you probably would not be considered for a $35,000 position. However, you could have the same set of credentials but be earning $30,000, and a firm might be glad to consider you an eligible applicant.

This type of thinking just cited is actually one of the most nearsighted practices of American business. The fact is that *accomplishments* are always a much better measure of talent than earnings. Fortunately, men and women in top positions are increasingly making personnel decisions according to this latter criteria.

When to State Your Present Salary

If your salary is relatively low, you should generally *avoid* stating it before an interview. Obviously you wouldn't want to negotiate from your present base, and divulging it in advance would only put you at a disadvantage.

There are some individuals who have conducted campaigns and negotiated offers without ever revealing their current income. However, there are few potential employers who will accept this type of negotiating position.

If you earn an exceptionally high salary for your age or experience, and if you are presently secure in a good position, then you might consider introducing it early in your discussions as a sign of your accomplishments. If you did not care to mention a figure, you could cite the *percentage growth* you have achieved over a specific period of time.

For most people, however, the guiding rule should be to avoid any financial disclosure or negotiation in the preliminary stages.

However, your strategy should include finding out what an employer hopes to pay and what range has been established.

Telling the Truth About Your Present Income

When it comes to financial matters, there can be little doubt that your competition will include some very imaginative liars. However, before you exaggerate your present level of earnings, you should be aware that it is very easy for an organization to check out your real income.

In actual practice, most firms *will not* seek a verification of present salary, and if you did exaggerate your earnings, you probably will survive. On the other hand, if anyone in the firm has reason to suspect your claim, they have a number of avenues open to them. Some of these are as follows:

1.   They may ask to see a payroll stub from your present employer.

2.   They may ask to see a copy of your last income or W-2 form.

3.   They may attempt to make a written or phone verification (after you have been hired) with your former supervisor and/or personnel department.

4.   They may rely on an outside agency for an investigation of your background and can perform a very accurate check of any earnings claim.

If you have a low salary and feel you must exaggerate to be considered for the position you seek, be sure to hedge in terms of an expected bonus or increase in salary. In other words, state your present income, but if you have a chance of shortly receiving an increase, be sure to make that level of earnings the basis for your negotiations.

Negotiating for Maximum Salary

If you are presently employed, I think that during the initial stages of your campaign you should maintain firm objectives. Start by shooting for what you believe you are worth and discipline yourself against letting people discourage you. Obviously, if you are unemployed or under immediate pressure to make a change, then this will affect the posture you take.

The following negotiation guidelines should prove of some assistance to most people.

Set attractive goals

Set optimistic goals for yourself and always sell "quality" rather than "low starting price." If you are looking to change for financial reasons, look for *at least* a 15% to 25% increase in net annual take-home pay.

This is particularly significant because people from $10,000 through $200,000 have won increases of 25%, 50% and even 100%. I'm not saying it is easy, but don't lower your goals without first testing your marketability over a couple of months.

Also, remember that if the potential employer meets your requirements, he will be looking for immediate acceptance of the job.

Win an offer before you start negotiating

Before you do any negotiating, you should always make sure that the employer is going to extend an offer. *Complete the sale before you try to close in on the exact dollars.*

Your first objective is to have an employer make up his mind on hiring you. If he isn't sure, premature financial discussions may turn him off.

Know the other person's alternatives

The finer art of negotiating requires some precise insight into the other person's *alternatives,* along with a knack for phrasing *your needs* so that they seem very reasonable.

Win sympathy for your situation

You should try to communicate the background to your thinking, and do this before you get to the stage where you are pinned down on a number. Make it easy for the employer to have some empathy for your situation.

Focus discussions on your short-term needs

During your discussions you should focus on standard of living and short-term, take-home pay...as opposed to gross annual income.

Negotiate a percentage increase

Also, depending on how much you are presently earning, it may be better to speak in terms of "percentages" instead of "thousands of dollars." It usually sounds like less.

Never accept offers on the spot

When you receive an offer, and regardless of how excited you may be, always ask for time to think it over.

If you decide you want the job, you should almost always try to negotiate a better package. An organization *is not* going to withdraw an offer just because you think you are worth more. The worst that could happen would be that they would hold firm on their original offer.

Be positive about everything but money

When you negotiate you should be absolutely enthused about everything but the financial part. I mean be *completely outgoing* in your excitement...about the firm...and about the future *opportunity*. In short, everything but the money.

Make sure the firm knows you'd love to start immediately. One easy way to introduce negotiation is to say that, after carefully reviewing your situation, the intangible costs of the move and other alternatives, you wish they could see their way through to meeting your needs. If that doesn't work, then try to get them to meet you halfway.

If your negotiation fails then try for "futures"

If you do not meet with any success in your negotiations, then you should shift from the "present," and instead focus on "futures." Here I am referring to a review after six months, a better title, an automatic increase after 12 months, etc. These are easier things for an employer to give.

Because of inflation, the whole area of salary negotiations has become more fluid. Guidelines have been set aside by employers in order to attract good candidates. Still, many people allow themselves to be deceived by discussions focusing on before-tax annual dollars.

From a financial standpoint, what you must be concerned with are the immediate and potential opportunities for improving your standard of living. Before accepting an offer, you should calculate just what an increase means in terms of "added funds on a weekly or monthly basis." This generally puts things into a much more meaningful perspective.

As a job seeker, your most difficult decision may involve the evaluation of "comparative offers." If you're young, or just starting out, the decision may be quite easy. In that case, *always put future opportunity over starting salary.*

If you are an executive, there is very little in the way of "rules of thumb" which can be provided. From personal experience, I have found that it does help to take the time to write *the positives and negatives of comparative offers* on paper. While it is convenient if the highest offer is also the most attractive opportunity, things rarely work out that way.

When you accept a job, you should always accept it verbally, and then *confirm your acceptance in writing.* The letter should restate your understanding of the key terms.

Contracts

It is very difficult to generalize about employment contracts. In recent years firms have taken a stronger stand against them. Their reasons for doing so are quite simple.

Contracts usually guarantee employees compensation for a certain length of time, as long as they work "to the best of their abilities in normal business hours."

Employers are guaranteed very little and the individual can usually break a contract quite easily. On the other hand, corporations are often forced into a settlement if they dismiss an executive under contract, and the courts favor individuals in these matters.

Despite corporate policies against contracts, it is difficult to conceive of any firm which would be willing to lose a sought-after executive simply because they want to maintain their policy.

A contract is just one more element in the total negotiation package. In any given situation a contract may be just as negotiable as questions relating to salary, bonuses, and stock option participation.

If you can possibly arrange it, a contract will usually be to your advantage. While you can always be dropped, a contract can provide you a measure of financial security and a certain degree of independence from corporate politics.

In many cases, having a contract may be the most significant *status symbol* that exists in a firm. For senior executives, a contract usually has a higher priority than the amount of salary. This is especially true if a corporation is likely to experience turnover in top management, or if a firm may be the target of an acquisition.

As a general rule, I feel that anyone above $40,000 should never be reluctant to ask for a contract. A request, as opposed to a demand, will never result in a revoked job offer, and there is a chance your request may be met.

However, you should be aware that your contract request may result in a number of negatively phrased comments. An employer may hint that your request reflects a lack of confidence in the firm, their management, or in your own ability. They may also ask you if you are the kind of executive who values security more than opportunity. You should anticipate comments such as:

"Your intense concern over a contract makes me wonder if you have the self-confidence and qualities which you've indicated. We're also very concerned about your trust in us. If our relationship is going to be as successful as we all plan, I think it should begin on a note of mutual trust and integrity."

As long as you anticipate them, these types of comments should be easy to finesse. There is usually only one major disadvantage that goes along with most contracts. If you request one, your employer may insist on inserting a protective clause which would *limit your ability to take future employment with a competitor.*

The insertion of such a clause is often requested as a show of good faith, and is quite hard to refuse without creating serious doubt in the mind of your new employer.

If you are at an executive level, there are certain companies with whom you must be very firm in your request for a contract. These would include: companies in financial trouble, firms that are merger or acquisition candidates or those which have just been merged or acquired, family controlled and private organizations, and companies where one individual personally dominates the environment.

In the above cases, you might consider seeking a three-year contract that covers your minimum compensation, and that also has provisions for such things as bonuses, deferred compensation, moving expenses, annual renegotiation upwards, and profit sharing.

You also may be able to negotiate such elements as life insurance, release with compensation in case of merger, salary benefits to your family in case of death, special reimbursement for foreign service, and out-placement marketing in the event of termination.

In any case, don't ever make the mistake of treating contract terms lightly and be sure to review all the fine print with a competent legal advisor.

Termination Agreements

In recent years, there has been a considerable increase in the use of "termination agreements." In most cases these are *substitutes* for employment contracts. Termination agreements are usually in the form of a short letter in which an employer agrees to an *irrevocable* severance compensation.

I personally favor the idea of these agreements and think that they can be devised to adequately serve the recruiting needs of most employers and the individual needs of executive job candidates.

In some industries, these agreements have already become quite common at salary levels above $50,000. However, I also know of a number of instances where people earning $40,000 have been successful in negotiating termination agreements.

In most cases, these types of agreements provide for a severance compensation of six months' salary, relocation expenses, insurance benefits for twelve months and professional outplacement. Any agreement that you accept should cover any and all situations under which an employer may choose to terminate your services.

The previous comments on contracts pertain to employment situations as they exist in the United States. If you are seeking a position in Europe, there is an entirely different environment.

Most European nations have enacted laws which are very much in the interest of the employee. In addition, employment contracts are quite common at relatively low salary levels. It is not unusual for a European company to give an individual two-years' notice prior to terminating his services.

Summary of Factors for Possible Negotiation

There are many forms of compensation other than base salary. The popularity of various methods fluctuates within industries, occupational specialties, and even with economic environments. Corporate perks, more properly known as perquisites, frequently cover assorted benefits which may or may not offer meaningful value to an employee.

Listed below are the major subjects which you might bring up in the course of negotiations.

base salary
sales commissions
bonus
profit sharing
expected income
expense accounts
medical insurance
life insurance
A.D. & D. insurance
vacations, free travel for spouse
company car or gas allowance
company sponsored van pool
use of vehicle in off hours
group auto insurance
stock options
matching investment programs
country club membership
annual physical exam
luncheon club membership
athletic club membership
disability pay
pension plan
legal assistance
adoption benefits

executive dining room privileges
financial planning assistance
overseas travel
C.P.A. and tax assistance
reimbursement of:
  moving expense
  mortgage rate differential
  mortgage prepayment penalty
  real estate brokerage
  closing costs, bridge loan
  trips for family to look for a home
  lodging fees while between homes
  shipping of boats and pets
  *installation of appliances/drapes/
    carpets*

mortgage funds
short-term loans
company purchase of your home
mortgage differential assistance
referred compensation
consumer product discounts
severance pay & outplacement
insurance benefits after termination

Salary Chart

This Annual Salary	This Monthly Salary	This Bimonthly Salary	This Salary Every Two Weeks	This Weekly Salary
10000	833	417	385	192
11000	917	458	423	212
12000	1000	500	461	231
13000	1083	542	500	250
14000	1167	583	538	269
15000	1250	625	577	288
16000	1333	667	615	308
17000	1417	708	654	327
18000	1500	750	692	346
19000	1583	792	731	365
20000	1667	833	769	385
21000	1750	875	808	404
22000	1833	917	846	423
23000	1917	958	885	442
24000	2000	1000	923	462
25000	2083	1042	962	481
26000	2167	1083	1000	500
27000	2245	1125	1038	519
28000	2333	1167	1077	538
29000	2417	1208	1115	558
30000	2500	1250	1154	577
31000	2583	1292	1192	596
32000	2667	1333	1231	615
33000	2750	1375	1269	635
34000	2833	1417	1308	654
35000	2917	1458	1346	673
36000	3000	1500	1385	692
37000	3083	1542	1423	712
38000	3167	1583	1461	731
39000	3250	1625	1500	750
40000	3333	1667	1538	769
41000	3417	1708	1577	788
42000	3500	1750	1615	808
43000	3583	1792	1654	827
44000	3667	1833	1692	846
45000	3750	1875	1731	865
46000	3833	1917	1769	885
47000	3917	1958	1808	904
48000	4000	2000	1846	923
49000	4083	2042	1884	942
50000	4167	2084	1923	962
51000	4250	2125	1961	981
52000	4333	2167	2000	1000
53000	4416	2209	2038	1019
54000	4500	2250	2077	1038
55000	4583	2292	2115	1058
56000	4666	2334	2154	1077
57000	4750	2375	2192	1096
58000	4833	2417	2231	1115
59000	4916	2459	2269	1135
60000	5000	2500	2308	1154
61000	5083	2541	2346	1173
62000	5166	2583	2384	1192
63000	5250	2625	2423	1211
64000	5333	2666	2461	1230
65000	5416	2708	2500	1250
66000	5500	2750	2538	1269
67000	5583	2792	2577	1288
68000	5666	2833	2615	1307
69000	5750	2875	2654	1327

Salary Chart

This Annual Salary	This Monthly Salary	This Bimonthly Salary	This Salary Every Two Weeks	This Weekly Salary
70000	5833	2916	2692	1346
71000	5916	2958	2730	1365
72000	6000	3000	2769	1385
73000	6083	3042	2808	1404
74000	6167	3083	2846	1423
75000	6250	3125	2884	1442
76000	6333	3167	2923	1462
77000	6417	3208	2962	1481
78000	6500	3250	3000	1500
79000	6583	3292	3038	1519
80000	6667	3333	3077	1538
81000	6750	3375	3115	1558
82000	6833	3417	3154	1577
83000	6917	3458	3192	1596
84000	7000	3500	3231	1615
85000	7083	3542	3269	1635
86000	7167	3583	3308	1654
87000	7250	3625	3346	1673
88000	7333	3667	3385	1692
89000	7417	3708	3423	1712
90000	7500	3750	3462	1731
91000	7583	3792	3500	1750
92000	7667	3833	3538	1769
93000	7750	3875	3577	1788
94000	7833	3917	3615	1808
95000	7917	3958	3654	1827
96000	8000	4000	3692	1846
97000	8083	4042	3731	1865
98000	8167	4083	3769	1885
99000	8250	4125	3808	1904
100000	8333	4167	3846	1923
101000	8417	4208	3885	1942
102000	8500	4250	3923	1962
103000	8583	4292	3962	1981
104000	8667	4333	4000	2000
105000	8750	4375	4038	2019
106000	8833	4417	4077	2038
107000	8917	4458	4115	2058
108000	9000	4500	4154	2077
109000	9083	4542	4192	2096
110000	9167	4583	4231	2115
111000	9250	4625	4269	2135
112000	9333	4667	4308	2154
113000	9417	4708	4346	2173
114000	9500	4750	4385	2192
115000	9583	4792	4423	2212
116000	9667	4833	4462	2231
117000	9750	4875	4500	2250
118000	9833	4917	4538	2269
119000	9917	4958	4577	2288
120000	10000	5000	4615	2308
121000	10083	5042	4654	2327
122000	10167	5083	4692	2346
123000	10250	5125	4731	2365
124000	10333	5167	4769	2385
125000	10417	5208	4808	2404
126000	10500	5250	4846	2423
127000	10583	5292	4885	2442
128000	10667	5333	4923	2462
129000	10750	5375	4962	2481
130000	10833	5417	5000	2500

CHAPTER 18

Developing an Outstanding Resume

In the 1980's, many millions of resumes will be circulated each year by job seekers. Given these numbers it would seem that the need for superior materials is obvious.

Nevertheless, the resumes circulated by most people are very poor. They are plain looking, either too short or too long for the individual's objectives, filled with dull, uninteresting words and characterized by errors such as misspelled words and uneven margins. Because of this, if you can develop an outstanding resume, you can gain an immense advantage over your competition. It will also pave the way for your creation of superior job search letters.

The Five Basic Resume Styles

Your resume will need to attract favorable interest and help generate interviews. It will serve as your personal advertisement, and can mean the difference between success and failure in obtaining the position you desire.

Your resume will also be the key to your development of superior job search letters. By preparing your resume first, it will be easier to select information for use in the letters you prepare.

Selecting the appropriate style of resume is important. There are five basic styles, and they offer different ways for arranging your background. Your choice will depend on which assets you have to emphasize and which liabilities you need to downplay. The five basic resume styles include:

Historical

This outlines your background in chronological order, beginning with your most recent position and working backwards in time. It is good for persons whose careers are an unbroken succession of increasingly responsible positions.

Functional

A functional resume organizes your experiences by function, such as marketing, engineering, etc., usually listing the strongest first. It is useful when a chronology might emphasize gaps in employment, frequent job changes or narrow industry experience.

Historical / Functional

This type of resume emphasizes functional strengths, but includes a chronological listing for credibility.

Achievement

Achievement resumes highlight outstanding accomplishments regardless of dates, company names or positions.

Situation

A more complex form of resume, this emphasizes situations (usually problems) and how you solved them. As with the achievement resume, it may not emphasize dates, company names or positions.

All resumes are either one of the five popular styles mentioned above, or a derivation of one of these types. However, before you attempt to select a resume style and begin writing, I suggest you review your goals, your data base of information about yourself, and your personal assets and liabilities.

Resume Construction

The resume is usually thought of as an introduction. It is supposed to create a desire on the part of an employer to see you. However, an effective resume plays a far greater role. For example, even after you have been interviewed, the chances are that your resume will be read again, perhaps by the individual who saw you as well as by others in the organization. A good resume will need to keep selling for you throughout the entire interview and negotiation process.

Accordingly, you should try to develop a resume that will appear alive and interesting to people at all levels. It should be a document which sells you without the reader being aware of or offended by the selling effort. The examples following this chapter will give you some ideas of the creative ways you can construct a resume. My own preference is for resumes which begin with the following major elements:

A short statement of your objectives

When possible, your resume should mention the positions that you are capable of filling. This accomplishes two important things. It gives the reader a feeling that you are a solid person who knows where he can be most effective. It can also enable a firm to rapidly spot a position goal that may coincide with a job they have available.

A summary of your main selling points

Most resumes describe only work experience. Your resume should be designed to sell both ability and experience. A brief but carefully worded summary can accomplish this for you. The use of both the objective and summary will help insure that your main selling points will be read. Here is an example which illustrates these two important points.

> **Objective** — *A position of senior sales and profit responsibility offering career opportunity as well as immediate challenge. Am particularly qualified to make a contribution as a Director of such functions as Marketing, Marketing Services, Planning and Marketing Development.*

Summary — *Am presently Director of Marketing with a division of a major drug corporation. Earlier, I was Senior Product Manager with a division of the same firm. Previous positions held with companies in the drug and appliance industries include Regional Sales Manager and Salesman.*

At 42 years of age, I am married and have an M.S. degree and a distinguished record as a Naval Officer. Personal qualities include creative and managerial skills, great initiative and an ability to get things done. Am well traveled and experienced at working with the highest levels of management.

The material which you will put into your resume can be generally categorized as either essential information or optional information. A brief commentary on each of these may be of some assistance to you.

Essential information includes your objective as well as personal data, education and experience. In almost all cases, these must appear in your resume.

Objective — Many people will face a difficult task in determining their job objectives. However, by the time you actually write your resume, you should have settled on your goals. With an objective mentally formulated, you now must put it in writing, and then prepare a resume which supports it.

Personal data — This includes your name, address and phone number. Other information should be included if it supports your objective. For example, age, sex, marital status, physical data and health would normally be listed.

Education — Be sure to highlight any educational information which supports your objective. Obviously, recent graduates must place more emphasis in this area.

In reviewing the information for inclusion in your resume, remember that all types of education are important. For example, you could consider using education obtained through military schools and company-sponsored courses.

Experience — This information is the core of your "sales presentation." It should show a potential employer what you have done, and what you are capable of doing. The key words are abilities, responsibilities and accomplishments. Stress those experiences which are most relevant and include specific examples of success.

To put your experience in perspective, you may also wish to include a brief description of your employers and their products or services. If confidentiality is necessary, you can omit the employer's name or other information which might reveal the firm's identity. Dates may also be left out, and it is best to omit salary information and your reasons for leaving past jobs.

Of most importance, the story you tell must strongly support your job objective. Cite any experience which helps you accomplish this goal, including reference to part-time, summer or volunteer work.

Optional information is anything which supports your objective while adding to the individuality of your resume. I suggest that you include any information which helps you build an image of being an interesting and well-rounded person. Some of the more common categories are listed below.

* Awards and honors
* Professional memberships
* Civic and social organization memberships
* Foreign language skills
* Travel experience

* Geographic and relocation preferences
* Patents and licenses
* Hobbies and interests
* Military service information
* Security clearances

Resume Copy

The copy in your resume must, of course, be well written. It should be interesting, with an emphasis on accomplishments rather than duties. The more you project your career as a series of potential benefits and progressive accomplishments, the more effective your resume will be.

These accomplishments should <u>be sales, profit or cost-control oriented</u> whenever possible. In listing your achievements, remember that this is not the time to be modest. You must use exciting words, which have some sell to them, and which can be handled in a manner that minimizes the fact that this is your opinion of yourself.

I've seen many opportunities lost by people who undersold themselves. Your aim is to present yourself in the most favorable light possible. You can be sure that your smart competition will be doing the same.

When it comes to writing, the words you choose can either add or detract from the impact of your qualifications. The phrases you select should tastefully convey a strong and genuine feeling. This is best achieved by using brief and direct descriptions, and by avoiding the temptation to be overly complex. Familiar words are the easiest to read and understand.

Make your writing personal and alive

Personalizing your writing will also help increase reader interest. This may require describing yourself to your reader in the first person and doing so without inhibition. The tone and style of your writing also plays an important role. A natural and warm tone combined with a crisp and clear style is best.

The use of "action" words is an effective technique for communicating benefits to a potential employer. Examples include words such as . . . developed . . . established . . . managed . . . planned, etc. The list included with our "Questionnaire for Resume Development" will aid you in assembling your own list of appropriate action words.

In preparing your resume copy, you should also use full descriptions rather than abbreviations. For example, American Management Association will have more impact than A.M.A.

Also, when referring to dollar figures, I suggest you write them out as numbers . . . $5,000,000 will usually have more impact than "five million dollars."

If your situation permits, you should always use exact chronological dates. This will add to your credibility.

Things to avoid

In attempting to create an effective resume, it is essential to use words with accuracy and precision. There are also a number of things you should be sure to avoid.

Clichés and wordy expressions such as "for the purpose of" and "in the event that" can be replaced by "for" and "if." Vague expressions such as "owing to the fact that" can be replaced by "because."

Also, grammatical errors and misused words will do little to enhance the professional image that you should project. For example, "irregardless," though frequently used, is not really a word.

Punctuation, capitalization and word divisions are the basics which will make your materials easier to read and understand. They are essential for creating a favorable impression on a potential employer.

Resume Graphics

One thing you must avoid is having a resume which looks just like every other average resume in circulation. This may sound very simple, yet it is something that is commonly overlooked. Its importance cannot be overstated.

The written materials which will attract maximum readership are ones that are clean and distinctive in appearance. Your written communications must all be attention-getters which are prepared in good taste, and which are simply more readable and attractive than competitive materials. To accomplish this, some things you might consider include the following:

Paper appearance

Since most people use white bond paper, I suggest you consider something different. A gray, ivory or off-white paper which has a textured or pebble finish, will stand out among any number of resumes. A paper of 20 to 24 lb. weight would be appropriate. Also, if you make use of back-to-back printing, be sure that the paper you select is sufficiently opaque to take printing on both sides without showing through.

Paper size and format

Since the size of your paper can add to the impression of uniqueness you may wish to consider preparing something other than the standard 8½" x 11" dimension. Obviously, there is no single best format. Some of the alternatives you could consider include:

> Monarch size stationery (7¼" x 10½") or, you might choose a 7" x 10", 6" x 9" or perhaps a 4" x 9" sheet which, when folded, would still fit nicely into a standard business envelope.

> You could also have your resume printed on both sides of 8½" x 11" paper, but then fold the paper into a 5½" x 8½" booklet. This can seem more personal since it makes your resume appear more like a letter. It also lessens the effect of overwhelming detail.

> Or, consider using an 11" x 17" sheet which folds over into an 8½" x 11" brochure. The cover page would have your name, address and phone number and perhaps your objective and summary.

Another variation of the above would be to start with legal-size paper, have it folded into three equal cuts, and utilize only five of the sides which are available for printing.

Margins and spacing

When using Monarch size stationery, be sure to leave ¾" to 1" margins on the left and right-hand sides, and a minimum of 1" margins on the top and bottom. Leaving sufficient <u>white space</u> will add to the dignity of your written materials.

When preparing a letter on 8½" x 11" stationery, leave side margins of 1" to 1½". The top of the page margins should be at least 1½" with the bottom margin allowing at least 1".

Type size and style

<u>A carbon ribbon will usually insure clear reproduction</u> of the typed resume. An IBM Selectric, or any standard typewriter with either Pica or Elite type, will prove adequate in most cases.

Most typewriters are known as being either 10 or 12-pitch typewriters. The term "pitch" simply refers to the number of characters typed per inch. When using Monarch size stationery, always use 12-pitch. For standard 8½" x 11" stationery, you can select either size, depending upon the amount of material you have.

If you want to do a particularly fine job, you could consider professionally typesetting your resume. <u>Nothing will look or read any better.</u> Typesetting would involve using an IBM Composer or any phototypesetter. These have wide ranges of distinctive type styles to choose from, and you will be able to get more words on each page.

For example, with the IBM Composer System you can select a reliable type which gives you 15 to 18 characters per inch instead of the standard 10 to 12.

In addition, you can make use of more than one type style in your resume. Captions and subheadings could be in a style which are different yet complementary to the ones used for your basic copy.

You can also vary the darkness of type according to three categories . . . light, medium, and bold.

If you decide to have your materials typeset, I suggest 11 point Univers Medium as a very readable and attractive type style. More detailed information on typesetting services is available from most printers.

Layout

The ideal resume page should be balanced and well organized. As previously mentioned, white space (the areas of your resume without type) can be used to add dignity, as well as highlight specific information and increase readability. I suggest you combine an appropriate amount of white space with the various division headings and sub-headings of your written material.

There are a number of ways to highlight information: italics, underscoring, bold type or asterisks or dashes before paragraphs. Use any of these sparingly, adding emphasis only where necessary. These techniques lose effectiveness if overused.

Also, be sure to avoid the use of illustrations, charts or graphs of any kind in your resume. They almost always detract from the overall dignity of the resume and give readers the impression that you are trying too hard.

Concluding Comments on Resumes

The importance of your resume is something which really cannot be overstated. One of your greatest advantages in your job campaign will be the fact that the average competitor will be using a resume which does not do his or her background justice.

By the way, this is not to say that those competitors will not be proud of their written materials. Most of them will have labored over the preparation of their resume and received numerous compliments from friends and relatives. However, this kind of approval has misled many talented people.

The fact is, there are few people whose opinions will be of value in judging the potential effectiveness of your resume. Even the typical resume produced by personnel professionals leaves a great deal to be desired.

Executives in the employment field will say that the best resume is one which presents the key facts enabling them to reach a quick decision. Unfortunately, your best interests may not be served by giving an employer a set of facts. The objective of your resume is to create an interest, even if you are not precisely sure of what the employer had in mind.

The most effective resume in helping you meet this objective will normally be one which is accomplishment-oriented. It must also sell your ability as well as your experience. It should be a resume designed to minimize the communication of your liabilities, and should be well-written.

A distinctive appearance, including selection of a good format, use of high-quality paper and typeset copy, will all greatly improve the readability of your resume.

For executives, a resume that closely resembles a letter is likely to be the most effective form of presentation. A Bio-Narrative resume (a biography in narrative form) presentation allows you to tailor your background, in effect building a statement which qualifies you for what you are seeking. Additionally, because it is similar to a letter, the communication seems more personal. A Bio-Narrative necessitates a superior level of writing skill. However, for executives, the potential benefit will be worth the effort.

Even if your resume meets the above criteria, there will be people who tell you that it isn't what it should be, that it is too long, or too short, that it's difficult to read or that it does not provide the facts.

What you need to do is simply produce the best document possible, given the advice at your disposal. If you are uncertain of the potential effectiveness of your resume, you can proceed to test it with a small distribution. In any case, if you follow the guidelines I have set forth, I am confident you will greatly increase your chances for success.

COLD TYPE EXAMPLE

The use of an IBM Composer or phototypesetter permits you to vary type styles, the number of characters per inch, the spacing between lines and the boldness of the lettering.

Type Styles (only a few of the available styles are illustrated)

This is an example of 11 Pt. Press Roman Medium
This is an example of 11 Pt. Baskerville Medium
This is an example of 11 Pt. Century Medium
This is an example of 11 Pt. Theme Italic Medium
This is an example of 12 Pt. Aldine Roman Medium
This is an example of 12 Pt. Bodoni Book Medium

Numbers of Characters Per Inch

This is an example of 8 Pt. Univers Medium
This is an example of 10 Pt. Univers Medium
This is an example of 11 Pt. Univers Medium

Spacing Between Lines

This is 10 Pt. Univers Medium typed solid
This is 10 Pt. Univers Medium typed solid
This is 10 Pt. Univers Medium typed solid

This is 10 Pt. Univers Medium typed 1 Pt. leaded
This is 10 Pt. Univers Medium typed 1 Pt. leaded
This is 10 Pt. Univers Medium typed 1 Pt. leaded

This is 10 Pt. Univers Medium typed 2 Pt. leaded
This is 10 Pt. Univers Medium typed 2 Pt. leaded
This is 10 Pt. Univers Medium typed 2 Pt. leaded

This is 10 Pt. Univers Medium typed 3 Pt. leaded
This is 10 Pt. Univers Medium typed 3 Pt. leaded
This is 10 Pt. Univers Medium typed 3 Pt. leaded

Boldness of Lettering

This is an example of 10 Pt. Univers Light
This is an example of 10 Pt. Univers Medium
This is an example of 10 Pt. Univers Bold

CHAPTER 19

Overcoming Liabilities

Almost any job hunter will have certain liabilities. If so, a communicative strategy should be established for dealing with them, and then applied in all written and interview communications.

Although it may seem obvious, you should always remember that employers seek to buy a maximum of assets and a minimum of liabilities. Since your initial objective is to get interviews, your resume and letters should disclose as few weaknesses as possible. During the interview, you then need to be ready to explain any negatives as it becomes necessary. The most common handicaps of individual job hunters include the following:

* Being young and inexperienced
* Being too old
* Needing to change careers
* Having experience which is very narrow
* Lacking a college degree
* Being unemployed

Being Young and Inexperienced

Individuals who think of their youth as a liability are simply indicating that others view their lack of experience as a negative, *relative* to their salary and position objectives.

Our experience has been that "youth" is the easiest of the frequently cited liabilities to turn into an asset. In your resume or letter, you will do best if you find some way to actually mention things like *interest in an industry, aggressiveness, drive, enthusiasm for a field, ability to learn quickly, and natural problem-solving talents.*

If you are short on work history, you will probably find a functional resume most effective. By highlighting a number of functions and skill areas, you will focus the reader's attention away from your years of experience and actual depth of achievements.

Of course, you would be wise to draw upon any part-time experience or extra-curricular accomplishments to profile your abilities. Comments on hobbies can also be used to effectively project an interesting type of personality and background. This is true whether the hobbies be car racing, sky diving, skiing, or bridge playing.

If you are young, "maturity" will be a key word. You must project yourself as someone who is a down-to-earth and solid type of person . . . someone who can make good, sound judgments in a variety of situations.

With rare exception, this will not be the time to present yourself as someone who "does his own thing." Also, as a general rule you will be wise to avoid extremes, emphasize career over immediate salary, and be specific in your preference for a type of job.

There is a growing number of companies with very young management teams, and they are willing to pay attractive salaries, regardless of a person's age. Because they are young executives themselves, they often seek talented young people for responsible positions.

If you are young, you should probably conduct a broader-than-usual job campaign. In the course of a large-scale campaign, you will be sure to reach the types of people mentioned in the previous paragraph.

If you happen to be a graduating student, I believe that virtually all of the strategy advice in this book will have application. Of course, students have the alternative of relying upon interviews through their college placement centers, and this is certainly a source to be used.

However, a concentrated direct employer contact will probably turn up job offers which involve more responsibility than the usual beginning positions with most large corporations.

For students interested in opportunities within small business, a full-scale campaign should be launched two months before graduation. This time schedule may seem very close. However, small businesses normally do not have training programs or other jobs which would be open for any length of time.

Being Too Old

It's always quite interesting for me to listen to the opinions which people express on age barriers and job hunting. In job seeking, older age can certainly prove to be a negative.

However, I think it is quite unfortunate that so many *unhappily* employed people believe they are too old to change jobs. Even though they may not consciously realize it, the truth is that many use age as a convenient excuse. Most of the time individuals either *lack the confidence to try, don't know how to go about it, or are not willing to go through the work a job campaign requires.*

At a senior age, winning a new job is never a simple task. The same holds true for settling into a different environment and becoming a success. However, despite difficulties in adjustment, and the stresses associated with proving yourself again, a good job change can bring you a totally new feeling about life. The excitement of new work, a new location, and new associates, may provide you with a mental stimulation that makes you feel ten years younger.

In the late 1960's and early 1970's, the job market seemed to be placing an ever-increasing emphasis on youth. For a while it seemed as though every business journal was relating stories about young millionaires and young presidents who met with rapid success. However, as a result of the mid-70's recession, there was a definite shift toward the favoring of experience over youth.

If you happen to be one of the people who thinks he is too senior-in-age, you might reflect on this for a second. At the same time, consider the fact that you must have accumulated experience which could be of value to literally hundreds, if not thousands of firms. Your major concern should not involve whether or not to seek a job. *The key question is simply how to communicate with the right people in the right companies.*

What does being too old really mean? In the United States half the population is over 27. To some people it is surpassing this number. In the job market, being too old actually has less to do with age than it does with responsibility and salary progress.

Being over 40, or even over 50, is far from being an insurmountable negative. To be sure, as you get older, job hunting will become more difficult, and particularly so in certain fields and industries. However, this is primarily due to the fact that as people rise up the organizational pyramid, there is a corresponding decrease in the number of available positions.

All age problems in job hunting are relative. Being too young could mean that you're 45 and shooting for a top spot in an industry where 90% of the top executives are 10 years your senior. On the other hand, being too old could be a case of being 32 in the advertising field and only earning $10,000.

Age really becomes a barrier at that point when you mentally *accept it as an obstacle.* Because of differences in fields and individual progress records, it is really impossible for anyone to state an age when things automatically become more difficult.

In terms of resume direction and content, many senior people struggle at condensing twenty or thirty years of experience into just two or three pages. After a great deal of work, the typical product of most efforts is a chronological history of many job descriptions.

Don't make the same mistake! Your focus should not be on chronological history, but should emphasize problems which you have faced and solutions which came about through your efforts. You should have very little difficulty finding a way to persuasively state some accomplishments which imply . . . *"I can do the same thing or more for you."*

In most cases you will have to rely more on letters than resumes, since information in letters can be more easily slanted to cover your age, length of experience and dates. You will find it useful to make a point of stressing your sound business judgment, your ability to work in any type of environment (with all levels of management), and your drive (which is, of course, what many believe senior people do not possess).

As far as your resume is concerned, you may wish to avoid mentioning your age. I would suggest that you emphasize only recent work experience (the last 10 years), and then disclose your age once you have an interview. You might also consider the use of a small and discreet photograph which projects a youthful image.

In terms of contacts, you should orient your campaign toward executives in your own age bracket or older. These people will obviously represent your best percentage chance. The birth dates of executives are included in many reference guides.

For example, *Dun and Bradstreet's Reference Book of Corporate Management* provides full background information on the officers of America's 2400 largest corporations. It covers dates of birth, colleges attended, previous employment, directorships held and other potentially useful information.

This is not to imply that you should avoid younger executives who will seek the complementary relationship which your age and maturity will bring. You may also have another advantage over some of them in that you are less likely to be viewed as a competitive threat.

The first impression a job hunter gives is always of critical importance. In fact, as I have previously emphasized, the first five minutes of many interviews are often more significant than all other minutes combined.

As you become older, your need to make a good first impression will become even more vital. If you're out of shape and run-down, start exercising, get some color in your face (either real or artificial suntan), consider dyeing your hair or getting a hairpiece, and investigate some of the more youthfully styled eyeglass frames.

You may feel uneasy about some of these thoughts, but if you really want to get a new job, they will give you a big advantage. Too often people worry about what associates will say when they see their new appearance. The fact remains that most of your potential employers will never have seen you before, and I have seen these efforts make the critical difference time and time again.

Needing to Change Careers

Many individuals who feel their age represents a problem will also be dealing with the special job hunting problems associated with *career changing*. In recent years, there has been great interest in this subject.

Because their abilities, interests and life styles have shifted, more people than ever are trying to change careers. In addition, many people have found themselves in overcrowded specialty areas with diminishing opportunities. For example, moves out of education, aerospace and defense fields have been very common.

While I am aware of many career change success stories, they are almost always the result of either careful planning or professional help. Otherwise, it may be impossible for you to achieve the responsibility level and income of your present job. Changing career fields is something that is never easy. In order to move into a responsible job in another field, most people need to have some related experience or education.

It is possible to train for another occupation by attending evening classes, graduate school programs and the like. However, this is always a time-consuming process, and educational credentials alone may still not solve your job search problem.

At the present time, there are literally thousands of occupations which experienced individuals could explore. Many individuals successfully expand hobbies into occupations. Some of the fields which have been recent favorites for those who were established elsewhere include the following:

college administration	manufacturer's representative
commercial art	executive recruiting
journalism	securities brokerage
photography	construction
interior design	social work
writing	university teaching
sales	franchising
exporting	music
local accounting	real estate
consulting	sports commentating
life insurance	painting
travel agencies	employment agencies
archaeology	market research
financial analysis	government positions
importing	(city, state, federal)
legal-related work	medical-related work

There are, of course, many hundreds of other occupational areas which individuals may wish to consider. If you find yourself in a position where you choose to launch a new career, you may find it worthwhile to talk to a professional counselor. At the very least, this may stimulate your mind in terms of the wide range of opportunities which are available.

The Federal Government also has numerous publications which provide information on the thousands of occupations pursued in America. The U.S. Department of Labor's *"Dictionary of Occupational Titles"* lists more than 30,000 classifications.

Another publication which will provide interesting information is the *"College Placement Handbook."* This gives data on the many fields and careers open to graduates and is published annually by the College Placement Council in Bethlehem, Pennsylvania. *"The Guide to U.S. Civil Service Jobs,"* published by the U.S. Government Printing Office in Washington, D.C. (20402) may also prove worthwhile.

When you are seeking work in an entirely new field, the job changing process becomes considerably more difficult. Your creative material must highlight those skills and facets of your experience which would be appropriate for the new field you wish to explore.

In your written communications, it will be important to break down your experience into functions common to all businesses, and skills that are utilized in the fields you wish to investigate. The key, of course, is to do this without over-identifying with your present industry or career field.

When you have interviews, your focus should be on showing the employer how transferable your skills are to his operations. Once again, enthusiasm for the industry and career field is vital.

When you are attempting a career change, the utilization of letters will prove far more productive than resumes. In fact, the normal avenues for seeking employment such as agencies, recruiters and answering ads, will not work very well for you. Our experience indicates that potential career changers have had unusually good results through contacting small businesses and by answering advertisements in the "business opportunities" sections of major newspapers.

If you happen to be fortunate enough to have capital available, you obviously can investigate starting your own business or buying a franchise.

As I mentioned, one key to making a successful career change involves sound career planning. If you have the time, you will be wise to begin studying, planning and working toward a goal while still in your current field. You should also seek assignments within your present organization which will help prepare you for other responsibilities.

With our changing educational environment, high divorce rate, and expanding communications in general, career shifts at almost any age are going to become more routine. By the middle 1980's, the maintenance of dual careers will become a common practice.

Having Experience Which is Narrow

If you have single industry or single company experience, you should consider using two resumes. One would be directed at the industry in which you have experience, while the other should be a functional resume which does not disclose the firm(s) or industry where you have spent your working life. An example of a functional resume is included in the resume section. In this type of resume, you must stress accomplishments by area of work. It also should make clear the kinds of benefits you could deliver to a prospective employer.

Having a Record of Too Many Job Changes

Job hoppers are people who have not shown much progression within companies, and who usually have a record of many lateral job changes. Almost any potential employer will be wary if this is your kind of record.

However, there is a big difference between job hoppers and those who have achieved great progress through changing jobs. There is certainly no stigma attached to the latter. Your job-changing will not be a liability if you can point to salary progress. In fact, there is no better evidence of employer satisfaction than a record of salary growth.

If you're afraid of being cited for too many job changes, a functional resume will again prove most useful. It will allow you to completely omit the names and number of companies with whom you have been associated.

Normally, your work history should appear in logical segments of your resume. However, in these cases the grouping of jobs within broader time frames would be a preferred alternative to listing each job and the dates of employment.

Your success in dealing with your record of job change will depend primarily on your reasons for leaving various situations. Acceptable reasons for leaving any employer include mergers or acquisitions; departure of talented superiors; a need for more challenge; changes in corporate growth policy; a desire to locate somewhere else in the country; and the extension of financial offers which were too attractive to turn down.

Lack of a College Degree

Though you may not have a degree, you should be able to cite some schools which you have attended, or perhaps correspondence courses, management seminars, military schools or some special training. If you combine this with statements that you have the ability to learn quickly, as well as creative, analytical or writing abilities, you will go a long way toward overcoming this liability.

In compensating for lack of a degree, the need for stressing accomplishments is also more significant than ever. You need to sell your job performance and try to find a way to emphasize that you are an educated and cultured individual. If you are an executive, an effective statement of accomplishments will almost always overcome any lack of formal education.

Being Unemployed

If you've just been fired, encouraged to leave, laid off, or otherwise dehired, the first thing to remember is not to panic. If you do panic, you are going to lose your confidence and ability to think clearly.

Being fired today is far from an unknown tragedy. It happens to corporate presidents and vice presidents all the time, and at a faster percentage rate than at middle management levels.

People may not admit it, and be quick to claim they quit all their previous positions, but it is likely that many executives who interview you will have shared the same experience at some stage in their career. In fact, it is a rare individual who can succeed in moving ahead without being fired at least once during his career.

Being fired, or asked to leave, doesn't mean failure in the eyes of everyone else, even though you may feel tremendously depressed. Don't let it give you a guilt complex, and even more important, don't feel sorry for yourself.

Most of the time people get fired because of a personality conflict, or because someone higher up demands a change due to pressures at that level. Other common reasons for terminations include cost reductions and acquisitions.

The first reason we mentioned is the most significant. This concerns those situations where people could not get along with their boss or at least not the way the boss wanted! There is a lot of truth in the saying . . . "choosing the right job is largely a matter of choosing the right boss."

Getting all the way to the top in most corporations requires as much *political finesse* as natural ability, and if you are a senior executive who has just lost at this game, all I can advise is that you sharpen your political intuition in the future.

Being unemployed does mean that you'll be carrying a handicap. Regardless of the circumstances, the great majority of firms prefer candidates who are presently employed. Nevertheless, every day people turn bad situations into greater success. Your ability to bounce back after a bad experience will be a true test of your basic strength and determination. If you are in this position, just take the advice in this book and really go to work on a campaign.

A common strategy of executives who are unemployed for a long period involves the creation of a consulting enterprise. This serves to provide continuity of employment. About all it takes is a phone, stationery, and a telephone answering service. *(An answering service will also sound far more businesslike than your family.)*

If you do find yourself in a position of having suddenly lost your job, I suggest the following:

Register for unemployment
Unless you have a lot of capital, don't let your pride stand in the way of accepting a weekly unemployment check. Almost everyone who loses a job ends up being unemployed for much longer than they expected.

Get a resume prepared and order stationery
The resume should look as though you prepared it before your termination, and should not reveal that your employment has ended.

Expect disappointment
Being an unemployed person means you will encounter false leads, generate unwarranted optimism and encounter more disappointment than ever. You will also be under emotional strain, and if you are out of work a long time, you may encounter family problems.

Don't vacation and don't hide

Start on your campaign immediately, exercise regularly and be as active as you can. Your great advantage will be your ability to devote your entire effort to job hunting.

Get access to an office phone

It helps to have a base of operations at an office. You might be able to use the number of a friend who can have his secretary take messages for you, or list a phone number (separate from your home phone) under your own consulting service.

Invest in your campaign

If you lose your job, start investing in your campaign right away. Even though you may be limited financially, the investment you make now will pay you back fifty times over. I also suggest that you complete a financial plan which assumes that you may be unemployed for the next six months.

In the course of planning, make sure that you eliminate all unnecessary entertainment and household luxuries. However, allow sufficient funds to enable you to dress well, to get any professional help you need and to actively pursue a first-class job campaign.

Don't be over anxious

Never beg for a position and never try to explain your present situation in print. Everyone likes to hire talent which is hard to find. Don't show up in advance of your scheduled interviews, and don't always be available at the first suggested time for further interviews.

Weigh your offers carefully

Even if your offers seem ideal, I suggest that you continue your campaign in full force for a few more weeks. This is pure and simple insurance. If something vastly superior develops, you can sit down and talk it over with your new employer.

Also, do not make the mistake of thinking you can always get a job at a salary cut. It can frequently be more difficult to get a lower paying job, for which you are over-qualified, than an equal or better position.

If you have been out awhile . . . revamp everything

Your new starting point should involve preparation of totally fresh materials. They should have an appearance and orientation which have little resemblance to your former materials. Slant a couple of resumes to different types of jobs which you could fill and make aggressive use of *telephone* and *direct mail* techniques.

At the same time develop *one standard letter* which incorporates your ability to fill these different types of positions and launch a mailing (with a resume) to every executive search firm and branch office possible. Don't worry about your materials reaching firms you've previously contacted.

CHAPTER 20

Examples of Letters

This section consists of letter examples. While fictionalized, they conform almost precisely to materials which proved effective for people seeking new positions.

When you review the letters, you should take a close look at opening and closing paragraphs as well as words these individuals have used in their attempts to persuade others. The examples that I have included are predominantly middle management examples. However, they will guide you regardless of your level or occupational area. While you shouldn't just copy them, you should be able to directly borrow words, phrases, sentences and paragraphs and adapt their use to your own background.

Letter Examples

For Contacting Employers:	*Letter example*
	Cover Letter example
	Third Party Letter example
For Answering Advertisements:	*Letter example*
	Cover Letter example
For Contacting Search Firms:	*Letter example*
	Cover Letter example
For Following Up Interviews:	*Letter example*

Sample of: Letter for Contacting Employers

Dear _____:

Your company's new emphasis on Industrial Relations was highlighted in this month's "Personnel Journal." I enjoyed reading this article and agree with many of the points that were made.

As a professional with 5 years' successful experience, I thought that my expertise in this field might be of interest to you.

In my present position as Regional Director with a $70 million firm, I have had full responsibility for implementing the Industrial Relations programs at our newly developed facilities in Chicago, Cincinnati and Detroit.

Some of my other recent accomplishments include:

... Designed the employee manual that is currently in use throughout the organization.

... Trained the individuals who are now directing personnel functions in Houston, Dallas, Los Angeles, and Seattle.

... Maintained superior labor relations in all plants. Not a single disciplinary action has been arbitrarily reversed during my tenure.

... Employee productivity and stability have been improved. Turnover in the plants I've set up is far below industry norm.

At 34 years and married with 2 children, I have a BA (1965) and an MA (1970) from Boston University. Relocation and travel requirements present no problem.

Confident that you would find a personal meeting both interesting and mutually profitable, I will call your secretary in a few days to arrange an interview at your convenience. I look forward to seeing if I can help with the exciting challenges you face.

Very truly yours,

Sample of: Cover Letter for Contacting Employers

Dear _____:

These are exciting times in the plastics industry. Stanco's plans for expansion have been widely publicized, and it's clear that things are really happening for your company.

Realizing that you cannot afford to waste any time, I'll get right to the point. I believe that I can make a solid contribution . . . immediately . . . as part of your Public Relations junior management team. Without intending to appear overly confident, here is why:

A recent cum laude graduate, I have worked for the last 3 years, on a part-time basis, as Assistant to the PR Director at Hayden and Co. My earnings there allowed me to finance my education.

In this capacity, I have been exposed to a variety of PR problems and have learned how to deal creatively with them. In the absence of a senior executive, I was recently given complete responsibility for company relations with minority groups.

Moving quickly, I have been able to improve our image among diverse segments of the community. To achieve this, I designed a series of seminars on what the company was doing, and how this could benefit the minority community as a whole.

At 22 years, I am single and interested in working with the kinds of challenges faced in the plastics industry. I have a BA in Business Administration from Fairleigh Dickinson University (3.1 out of a possible 4.0).

Enclosed is a copy of my resume. If you can use someone with my talents and enthusiasm, I would appreciate the opportunity to speak with you personally.

Very truly yours,

Sample of: Third-Party Letter for Contacting Employers

Dear _____:

It's not often that I feel compelled to write on behalf of a business associate. In this case, it's a pleasure. Impressed by your company's steady growth, he has expressed the desire to relate the benefits of his expertise to your needs.

Employed within your industry, he is presently a Manager of Finance. A few of his accomplishments are outlined below:

* Developed the company's first corporate 5-year plan.

* Computerized budgets for 15 profit centers, and improved sales forecasts to a 90% accuracy through use of mathematical models.

* Saved 30% in labor costs by overhauling the accounting system and developing a complete Procedures Manual.

* Contributed to a 40% increase in profits by providing the sales force with previously unavailable market information on more than 5,000 products.

Originally from England, he holds a BA in Economics and an MBA from Cornell. He is fluent in English, German and French. Dedicated, ambitious and capable, his other qualities include excellent communication skills and an ability to motivate subordinates.

I can highly recommend him as a valuable team member for any growth company. Enclosed is his resume for your review. If you decide that an interview would be desirable, I would be delighted to arrange it.

Very truly yours,

Sample of: Letter for Answering Ads

Dear _____ :

National CSS is a recognized leader in the EDP industry. Your advertisement for a Systems Manager encouraged farsighted individuals to contact you. This is my reason for writing. Over 10 years of professional experience have allowed me to gain valuable expertise. The following summary of my qualifications should testify to this claim.

As a Project Manager . . .

Was responsible for justification, design and implementation of on-line systems at the NYC corporate HQ's of a $2 billion manufacturer. Installed a customer master system and an on-line system to better utilize the firm's 4,000 vehicles.

As a Senior Systems Analyst/Project Leader . . .

Spearheaded conversion to OS/CICS and supervised 10 analysts. Also implemented worldwide use of this system, traveling throughout the U.S., Europe and Asia. Contacts ranged from junior trainees to Executive Vice Presidents.

As a Supervisor . . .

Installed a Honeywell 600 system and implemented payroll, accounts payable and general ledgers for a large municipality. Controlled a $250,000 budget, reporting to the Director of Finance.

At 45 years and in excellent health, I am married with 2 children. I hold a BBA from Rutgers University (1956) and am a graduate of the Control Data Institute (1966) for systems & programming.

At the present time, I am seeking a new challenge — one where my innovative talents can be applied. Your company seems to offer such a challenge and my credentials match your requirements. I look forward to hearing from you.

Sincerely yours,

Sample of: Cover Letter for Answering Ads

Dear _____ :

I found myself challenged by your advertisement inviting talented engineers to apply for your position of Project Leader. My qualifications match your stated preferences.

For the last 13 years, I have worked for General Electric. When I first joined in 1965, they were just starting up an X-ray division. In the course of our growth, I have been given increasingly responsible positions, and presently enjoy a Senior Project Leadership role.

My accomplishments in the last year include:

. . . Initiated a make/buy evaluation involving a high speed rotor controller. Results: improved performance and $500,000 in annual savings.

. . . Re-evaluated an X-ray tube program against changing market demands. Results: the program was cut, saving $600,000 in potential redesign costs.

Throughout my career, my superiors have recognized my personal commitment, creative talents and ability to meet whatever objectives were assigned.

Enclosed you will find a resume which provides a comprehensive summary of my experience and achievements. Realizing that a written biography cannot adequately communicate the benefits I can provide you, I would appreciate the opportunity to speak with you personally.

Yours truly,

Sample of: Letter for Contacting Executive Search Firms

Dear _____:

1981 will be a difficult and challenging year for most firms. If one of your clients is faced with problems in their international operations, I may have qualifications which can help solve them.

My 15 years of engineering and management experience have included a series of increasingly responsible positions. Most recently, I have managed three foreign subsidiaries for American Can Company. A few areas of current responsibility include:

P&L Responsibilities . . . for 3 of American Can's overseas entities, with individual sales volume to $9 million.

General Management Responsibilities . . . for all company functions including finance, sales and manufacturing.

Engineering Management Responsibilities . . . including research and development, and engineering review of all efforts.

Negotiation of Contracts . . . with U.S. and foreign governments as well as major corporations.

Now I am seeking a new association with a company which can benefit from my years of executive experience. Married, with one child, I have traveled extensively throughout Europe, South America and the U.S. Also, I possess a BS degree in Industrial Engineering from the University of Michigan and am a registered Professional Engineer. My compensation needs exceed $50,000.

In the course of an interview, I would be pleased to discuss how I could be of potential value to your clients. I will call your office next week.

Sincerely,

Sample of: Cover Letter for Contacting Executive Search Firms

Dear _____ :

In the course of your search assignments, you may have a requirement for an accomplished Sales Manager.

My career has covered responsible positions with 3 blue chip firms: Ward Foods, Gulf & Western Industries and The Procter & Gamble Company. I have substantial experience in the food, detergent and motion picture industries.

In all of my assignments I have worked closely with Corporate Officers, as well as with their leading consulting firms, on a wide range of trouble shooting and sales management assignments.

My ability to define problems, develop alternatives and implement solutions, has brought praise and respect from my professional associates.

The enclosed resume briefly outlines my sales achievements over the past 17 years. Depending upon location and other factors, my salary requirements would be between $40,000 and $50,000.

If it appears that my qualifications meet the needs of one of your clients, I would be happy to further discuss my background in a meeting with you.

Cordially,

Sample of: Follow-Up Letter to an Interview

Dear _____:

Our discussion last week was very exciting. This letter is to summarize my background and its relevance to your requirements for a profit-oriented Vice President of Marketing.

Upon my arrival at Delmonico in 1968, marketing efforts were at a standstill. The operating units of the company were undirected and floundering. Sales revenues were just over $100,000,000.

By utilizing a wide range of creative and management talent, I acquired three firms, introduced a dozen new products and forged a new identity and communications direction for Delmonico. Today, the company is approaching the $1 billion mark, largely as a result of the marketing department's programs.

Through my personal involvement in Public Relations, the company has also won acclaim for its annual reports for the last 5 years.

Having enjoyed a successful career with Delmonico, my abilities have now outpaced the present challenges available with the firm.

Your company's needs are of continuing interest to me. I have little doubt that if given the opportunity to work for you, I can make an immediate and substantial impact in the marketing area.

Needless to say, I would enjoy exploring your requirements further. If I can be of any assistance in clarifying what I can offer, please feel free to contact me.

With best regards,

CHAPTER 21

Examples of Resumes

This section consists of resume examples. While fictionalized, they conform almost precisely to materials which have proved effective for people seeking new positions.

When you review them, you should take a close look at the layout of each resume. In addition, be sure to note the types of information which these individuals have decided to communicate. The examples that we have included are predominantly middle-management examples. However, they will guide you regardless of your level or occupational area.

Examples which are illustrated:

> *Historical resumes*
>
> *Functional resumes*
>
> *Historical/Functional resume*
>
> *Achievement resume*
>
> *Situation resume*

Historical Resume

ANTHONY MACMILLIAN
17 Maple St., Newton, NJ 07860 201-728-8153

OBJECTIVE

Executive Designer

PERSONAL

Born 8/21/29, married, two children, excellent health, U.S. citizen.

EDUCATION

Rhode Island University - BS in Industrial Design, 1959.
UCLA MS in Industrial Design, 1963.

PROFESSIONAL EXPERIENCE

Creative Design   **1969 — Present**
Newton, New Jersey

Executive Designer and Product Development Head. Created art-oriented children's discovery kits for nationally advertised subscription series. Designed puzzles, games, manipulatives and storage units in support of a unique elementary school teaching system. Conceived and developed new toys, and redesigned old ones to meet stringent market requirements. Successfully directed over 40 designers.

Concord Electronics   **1966 — 1969**
Garden City, New York

Section Head in the Creative Development Department. Directed a team of engineers, industrial designers, draftsmen. Designed electronic equipment under Federal, industrial, military and Space Agency contracts. Specialized in designing for volume production where cost control, sophisticated engineering and contemporary image were all important.

Page Two.....Anthony MacMillian

Dayton Mfg. Co.   **1954 — 1966**
Wayland, Massachusetts

Senior Engineer and Group Head. Responsible for the mechanical engineering and industrial design of electronic consoles, equipment cabinets, computer modules and data display devices. Assignments covered all aspects of R&D from mock-up stage to manufacturing follow-through and environmental testing.

McClennen & Jones   **1952 — 1954**
Architects
Albany, Georgia

Specified all interior colors and finishes for schools and office buildings. Designed lobby murals, mosaic tile walls, custom auditorium seating and stage curtains. Selected furnishings and customized kitchen equipment.

Westinghouse Electric Co.   **1948 — 1951**
Home Appliance Division
Pittsburgh, Pennsylvania

(Interrupted by military service as naval officer)

Performed time and motion studies, established piece-rate standards for production of home electric appliances. Underwent management training and became labor relations assistant investigating grievances and negotiating wage rate disputes.

GENERAL

Creative, resourceful, sensitive, purposeful, adaptable.

EARNINGS

My motivation in seeking a new position is primarily financial. While I have enjoyed excellent progress in my present position, I believe my achievements have far exceeded my possibilities for financial growth.

REFERENCES

Supplied upon request. Please do not contact former employers until a mutual interest has been established.

Historical Resume

Martin Wethersbee   74 Sycamore Ave., Louisville, KY 24101
(415) 621-8336

Objective: **Chief Financial Officer**

Background Summary: A Financial Executive with an extensive background in cost controls, budgeting, profit planning, competitive price analysis and forecasting.

Also author of a leading textbook on Corporate Finance; active as a fund raiser for major universities, and a counselor to professional athletes.

Major Conglomerate (1971-Present)   **As Vice President Finance**

— Monitored and negotiated the final closing on a $25 million cash acquisition.
— Renegotiated loans totaling $20 million.
— Extended credit lines with vendors to double accounts payable level without serious adverse reaction.
— Initiated control programs resulting in 18% reduction in inventory levels.
— Directed the evaluation of facility realignments and proposed mergers.
— Assisted divisional managers in management problems.

Penn Corporation (1968-1971)   **As Division Controller**

— Directed the evaluation of profitability for a number of consumer and industrial products on both variable and fixed contribution bases.
— Recommended plant closing which reduced assets employed by $2,500,000 and improved profits by $500,000 a year.
— Installed a budgetary program and reporting system to provide effective control of product line profits and manufacturing costs.
— Directed the financial evaluation of proposed acquisitions.
— Experienced functional supervision over the Controllers in five operating plants.
— Assisted general manager on a major turn-around.

General Foods
(1964-1968)

As Division Controller
— Directed all financial activities at G.F.'s largest manufacturing facility which had sales of $200 million and 4900 employees.

— Counseled management on the development of operating plans, performance reports, variance, analyses and evaluation of operating alternatives.

As Manager - Pricing Analysis
— Exercised functional supervision over all cost accounting, cost estimating and manufacturing expense budgeting activities in the Corporation.

— Installed a program for competitive price analysis and directed the development of end product prices.

Coca-Cola Co.
(1958-1964)

As Supervisor - Cost Accounting
— Exercised functional supervision over cost accounting activities in 43 manufacturing plants (7 divisions) of the Corporation. Also developed and installed direct and indirect labor control programs.

As Staff Assistant/Manufacturing
— Evaluated the financial implications of varied operating problems.

— Participated in the development of budgeting and profit planning programs; guided operating divisions in the implementation of these programs.

Corn Products
(1953-1958)

As Cost Analyst
— Worked at the plant level and at the division staff level in financial control activities, including budget development, performance analysis and reporting, forecasting, facilities studies and operational analysis; also developed and installed a standard cost accounting system.

Education: Emporia University Bus. Adm.-Acctg. Major
3.6 Average - 4.0 Basis

Personal: Height - 6'   Weight - 180
Married - 1 child

Functional Resume

William Cross   168 East 60th St.,   New York, NY 10022   212-726-3463

**General
Background**

Experienced general management executive with a record of over 20 years proven accomplishments in the areas of sales, marketing, personnel, production and purchasing.

Have held a wide variety of jobs and progressed from Foreman through Vice President with responsibility for the complete management of sales/profits for a major division.

Am widely traveled and willing to relocate. Presently 46 years old. Education includes study at the University of California. Military service consisted of 4 years in the U.S. Army (discharged as Captain).

Personal attributes include dedication to a job . . . the ability to effect strong loyalty from subordinates . . . effectiveness in working independently or as part of a team . . . capacity to get things done . . . and, the managerial skill to meet stringent production, sales or cost objectives.

Areas of Major Experience

Personnel

Have been responsible for large-scale work forces . . . union and non-union, technical and administrative. Have had full authority for all hiring and termination, the execution of union negotiations and responsibility for salary administration.

Numerous accomplishments in managing a staff skillfully. Proven ability for inspiring loyalty and minimizing absenteeism, turnover, and serious labor problems.

**Sales/
Marketing**

Have been responsible for a sales organization which generated a volume of $7,000,000. During a 5-year period, sales and profits were tripled.

Opened new markets for products through contacts on a direct basis with chains.

Page two   **William Cross**

Conducted continuous <u>market research</u> which was oriented toward expanding distribution of food products normally sold along ethnic lines.

Personally developed <u>sales promotions</u> and associated point-of-purchase materials. Directed various promotions under widely varying circumstances.

Have <u>strong personal contacts</u> with officers and owners of various chains including firms such as A&P, Jewel Tea, Finast, Safeway, Penn Fruit, etc.

Production   <u>Widely experienced in managing production output and problems.</u> Previous positions held include Foreman — Production Supervisor — Plant Manager.

Have a record of accomplishments in all of the above positions. Some examples are the following:

(1) Frequently overhauled production schedules and coordinated work between shifts to effect significant savings in time, direct labor, and overhead costs.

(2) Initiated sweeping quality and product controls which led to superior performance.

(3) Introduced systems of cost and price controls and insured their useful implementation.

Purchasing   <u>Have been responsible for the purchasing function.</u>

Assisted in the design of new plants in major cities. These included facilities for production, warehousing, and shipping.

Introduced quality control reports permitting guides to be established for bulk purchasing.

Provided guidance to Plant Managers on problems involving pricing and inventory control.

Instituted procedures and controls which guaranteed the availability of diverse materials to meet critically timed production schedules.

Functional Resume

BURNS GOFFREY,   423-B Steelton Street
Denver, Colorado 80205
(303) 771-4454

Research Executive with responsibilities including conception, preparation, execution and presentation of research surveys and sales analysis projects.

Summary: 14 years diverse experience in performing sound and creative market research and communicating it to management. Skilled in consumer media research, sales analysis and product testing. Experienced at working with salesmen, sales promotion and advertising executives. Have engaged in every phase of the survey operation from field interviewing to presentation.

Some Related Accomplishments

Presentations: Written & Verbal	Have written and presented research reports on such topics as: effectiveness of point-of-purchase advertising; food, beverage and tobacco usage; rail express shipments; magazine and newspaper editorial readership; and sales audits in retail outlets.
Planning Organizing Coordinating	Devised survey samples. Developed and pre-tested questionnaires. Performed and directed field interviews. Supervised editing, coding, and tabulation of survey results.
Training Supervision	Trained and supervised interviewing crews for specialized field studies in 21 metropolitan areas in 18 states. Validated and edited their work. Instructed and supervised office personnel in techniques of report tabulation.
Technical Knowledge	Thorough knowledge of statistical techniques and linear programming. Familiar with the operation of I.B.M. equipment.

Promotion	Wrote several membership promotional booklets containing complete descriptions of association services and activities. Composed copy for sales promotion literature and answered mail and telephone inquiries for trade associations and publications.
Follow-through	Developed system to expedite processing of magazine reader service cards used to order literature from advertisements, catalogs, and new product announcements. Issued monthly reports on advertising pages' breakdown for numerous competitive trade journals. Computed liquor consumption figures for all U.S. markets.
Personal	37 years old, 6'5", 210 lbs., single, excellent health.
Education	B.S. degree in Economics, Miami University.
Employment History	Assistant Marketing Director Roberts Advertising Agency, 1964-67 Associate Research Director Hartman Publishing Corp., 1962-64 Project Director J.E.L. Steel Company, 1960-62 Field Manager Western Foods Inc., 1954-59 Market Analyst Audits & Surveys, Inc., 1952-54 United States Air Force, 1949-51
Organizations	American Statistical Society Lions International

Historical / Functional Resume

J. Marcus Bernstein   41 Elm Road, Bronxville, NY 10552   (212) 682-4731

EMPLOYMENT HISTORY

7/1970 to Present . . . . LTV, Inc. — N.Y.C. Sales $20,000,000.
Manufacturer of tape equipment and pre-recorded tape cartridges.
Position: Assistant to the Executive Vice President.

4/1967 to 7/1970 . . . . Jarvis Radio — Div. of Magnavox Corp., Bethpage, NY. Sales $6,400,000.
Manufacturer of hi-fidelity components and communications equipment.
Position: Sales Manager promoted to General Manager.

6/1965 to 3/1967 . . . . B.P.I. Technical Communications — White Plains, NY. Sales $2,000,000.
Manufacturers of Citizens Band two-way radio equipment. Position: National Sales Manager.

EXPERIENCE

Sales . . . . Successfully sold dozens of different products. Considerable volume with premium users as well as catalog and stamp plant firms. Import/export experience. Direct mail know-how. Knowledge of distribution patterns in electronics.

Sales Promotion . . . . Formulated advertising budgets and campaigns. Designed p.o.p. materials, displays, racks and exhibits. Prepared literature, catalogs and service manuals. Working knowledge of the graphic arts. Participated in and supervised numerous trade shows.

Product Development . . . . . . Determined product desirability in the marketplace. Involvement at most levels of product design. Liaison with engineers, designers and production personnel. Knowledge of patent and trademark regulations.

Management . . . . Formulated corporate policy and marketing programs. Hired, trained and supervised field sales personnel. Managed manufacturing facility employing hundreds. Prepared stockholders reports.

Personal Data . . . . 34 years of age, single, 6'3", 195 lbs.
College: N. Y. U., 3 years, evenings.
Industrial Distribution Major. "A" student.
Veteran: U.S.A.F., 3 years, Air Control
Determined, innovative, versatile, personable, a driver.
Effective in attorneys' offices, union negotiations, board meetings, shirt-sleeve confabs, or Tokyo factories.
Seasoned traveler...500,000 air miles.

Achievement Resume

Tom Donaldson   83 River Road   Cleveland, OH 44131   216-447-0955

Public Relations Director

Public Relations - Promotion Specialist, Expert in Industrial Communications. Thirteen years broad-range experience with three major industries. Presently Senior Writer / Editor with a major defense company.

- Earned 17 awards including four consecutive Freedom Foundation awards; citations from International Council of Industrial Editors, Treasury Department, Manufacturing Chemists Association; plaques from the Detroit Advertising Club and California Public Relations Association.

- More than 350 articles published.

- Designed, wrote and taught courses in Creative Thinking at major defense company. Lectured on Communications and Creativity to many organizations, including Central California Industrial Editors, Toastmasters International Industrial Management Club, and Florida Scholastic Association.

- Started community newspaper for Civic Center, continuing as Editor. Own a free-lance public relations promotion business called Creative Communications. Accounts include: Mid-California Technical Institute, City of San Diego, San Diego Chamber of Commerce, Loch Haven Art Center, Jonny Bremer's (Putt-Putt Pizza, Chug-Chug Chicken), Swanky Franky, and Creativeering Associates.

- Active member of Public Relations Society of America, National Management Association, Toastmasters International, Sigma Delta Chi, International Council of Industrial Editors; Vice President of Central California Industrial Editors Association, Program Chairman and Editor of monthly newsletter; Associate Editor of *WESTERN ACCENT,* regional publication of Western Council of Industrial Editors.

- Completed 18 courses in writing, publicity, public relations and advertising since 1953. Attended numerous management conferences. Recent conferences include: Miami Conference on Communications Arts, University of Miami, April 1975; Editors Conference at University of Florida, November, 1976; Quest for Creativity, Oneida State University, August 1979.

- BSJ degree at Northwestern School of Journalism, February 1953. Voted "Outstanding Journalism Graduate" — awarded Sigma Delta Chi Special Award.

- Married, two sons. Formerly Captain —U.S.A.F.

Situation Resume

Paul Carlson   44 Devon Road   Essex Fells, NJ 07021   (201) 226-7148

General Management / Sales Executive

An IBM executive, my most recent assignment has been to revitalize a $50,000,000 multi-location activity which employed 815 persons. My job was to rebuild profitability. In less than 6 months, I reversed the downward trend, established a new marketing concept ..and eliminated manufacturing bottlenecks. In addition to a $4,500,000 gain in profits, revenue advanced by 45%.

Earlier, I held P&L responsibilities as General Manager of a new operation. In this position my efforts drew praise from top executives throughout our $20 billion corporation. As a result, I was awarded IBM's most prestigious management honor, "The President's Trophy."

Previously, as District Manager in the lowest-ranked GEM district in the nation, I was instrumental in our growth to top positions 24 months later...with sales increasing by $50,000,000. Prior assignments included responsibilities as Product Marketing Manager at our $800,000,000 regional headquarters, and as Sales Manager responsible for a 75-man team of engineers and representatives in the Los Angeles area.

Starting in sales, my rise through the ranks began early. I earned initial supervisory responsibilities in less than 3 years. My personal background includes an M.B.A. from Harvard, and a B.A. from Amherst. I am 47 years old, in excellent health and physical condition, and married with 3 children.

I joined IBM in 1966 when the Data Processing Division was still in its infancy. Since then I have participated in one of the most complex expansions ever engineered by a U.S. corporation. A few highlights of my overall career are indicated as follows:

Revitalization and Expansion of a $50,000,000 Operation

It was in mid-1976 that my attention focused on an unusual situation within the company. Headquarters' staff had tentatively decided to discontinue one of our established operations. Both revenue ($50,000,000) and profit had been falling for an extended period of time. In spite of their cautions, I promoted the concept of reorganization.

page 2...Paul Carlson

Once my plans were approved, I moved rapidly on a number of fronts. At the outset, I reduced the 815-person staff by more than 15%, eliminating duplication of effort in all departments. In addition, I shifted our basic marketing strategy which allowed us to substantially increase revenue. Then, working closely with our controller, I tightened controls in all areas. By year end, a full profit recovery was clearly established...up by more than $4,500,000. Sales had increased 45%.

New Business Startup
in Los Angeles

As corporate growth continued to accelerate throughout the late 1960's, I was charged with responsibility for opening a new office in the Los Angeles area. After an exceptionally fast startup, we entered some of the toughest years ever experienced by the Data Processing Division.

It was against this backdrop that I launched a 5-year plan destined to rank my organization among the top performing offices in the country. When all was said and done, we employed 15 managers, more than 100 support personnel, with revenue reaching $33,000,000 per year by 1975. Our consistent ability to meet revenue and expense targets, coupled with long-range planning effectiveness, led to personal performance ratings of "rarely ever achieved."

Building the Northwest Area
of the United States

When appointed as second in command of this $220,000,000 district, it was recognized that annual sales were not up to the company's traditional expectations. During my 24-month assignment, I coordinated 15 major offices throughout the northwest. My direct responsibilities included marketing, accounts receivable, planning and product objectives as well as the preparation of sales quotas and special promotions. Additional duties included recruiting, education and resource allocation.

One of our major accomplishments was moving this district from a 7th ranking nationally in 1970, to 1st ranking in 1971. This was an intense effort targeted against 24 quantitative objectives. By the end of my tenure, we had organized the entire staff into an efficient team-oriented operation.

CHAPTER 22

Developing Your Data Base/ Questionnaire for Resume Development

Most people find it very difficult to sit down and actually develop their resume. This is because they try to move directly into the "writing phase." As part of this system, I suggest a fairly basic four-stage process that should make it easier for anyone to draft their materials.

The 1st stage is development of your data base. Collect all ideas and historical facts which might be of any conceivable value. To help you with this I have designed a questionnaire that is adaptable to all types of situations.

The questions themselves will help elicit a maximum amount of pertinent information about you. They will also help you recall factors which might otherwise have been forgotten. Furthermore, if you think you don't have enough material for a resume, then a listing of verbs on the seventh page should stimulate your thinking. Once completed, it can serve as a permanent personal history record.

The 2nd stage is a review of the material you have just collected. A few days after completing the questionnaire, I suggest that you take a fresh look at everything you have written. You will probably find that you have some additional ideas you wish to include.

The 3rd stage involves selecting a resume style that highlights your assets and minimizes communication of any liabilities. Then you need to sketch out your resume format.

When you do this, use a pencil to sketch headings in the exact positions in which they should appear on your finalized resume. After establishing the framework, draw lines in those areas where you plan to include the body copy.

In the 4th stage you will actually write the copy. However, because you have organized the format in advance, you should find it easier to judge the amount of copy you need for each category in your resume format.

Now, carefully review the data base questionnaire on the following pages. Before beginning, however, gather the records which will enable you to complete these forms easily. Personal, education, military and employment information should all be fully recorded.

The time you invest in completing these forms will be of significant value, both now and in the future. When you write the copy for your resume, the data base will provide a current, organized reference source. Later, the data base can be readily updated by adding information about subsequent positions, responsibilities, education or activities.

General Data

Name: _____

Address: _____

_____

Phone #:   Home: _____ Bus: _____

Date of Birth: _____

Height: _____ Weight: _____

Marital Status: _____ Children: _____

Language Facility

(Indicate excellent, good, fair, etc.)

(Language) (Speak) (Read) (Write)

_____ _____ _____ _____

_____ _____ _____ _____

_____ _____ _____ _____

_____ _____ _____ _____

Travel & Relocation:

Extent of Previous Travel: _____
(countries, area of U.S.)

Willing to travel? (%) _____

Willing to relocate U.S.? _____   Preference: _____

Willing to relocate overseas? _____   Preference: _____

Education:

Degree or % Completed & Year	(School)	(Concentration)	(Class Rank)	(Grade Point Average)*
BA, BS, etc. _____	_____	_____	_____	_____
MA, MBA, MS, etc. _____	_____	_____	_____	_____
PhD, LLB, etc. _____	_____	_____	_____	_____

If better than average achievement in concentration, please indicate

Courses taken in school
relevant to your occu-
pational objectives: _____

_____

_____

Scholastic honors,
scholarships,
assistantships, etc.:   _____

_____

_____

Extra-curricular activities, achievements, etc.: _____

_____

_____

_____

Extent of work while in school: (name of company, summer work and % of educational expenses earned) _____

_____

_____

_____

	Title of Course	Conducted By	Dates Attended
Additional professional training: (seminar, conferences, training programs, correspondence courses, etc.)	_____	_____	_____
	_____	_____	_____
	_____	_____	_____

Present Interests/Activities

Professional society or business association memberships, offices held committes served on: (also articles, publications, copyrights, patents, inventions, etc.) _____

_____

_____

_____

_____

Civic/political organizations, memberships, offices held: certificates, professional licenses held, etc. _____

_____

_____

_____

Principal recreational activities: (athletic, hobbies, etc.) _____

_____

Military Service

Branch of Service: _____

Date Entered: _____ Rank: _____

Date Discharged: _____ Rank: _____

Highest Rank Held: _____

Reserve Status and Rank: _____

Specialized training _____
schools, etc. type/
length of time: _____

_____

_____

_____

_____

_____

Military Assignments:

_____ *Responsibilities* _____

Place	Titles (Specialty)	Men	Budget	Material
_____	_____	_____	_____	_____
_____	_____	_____	_____	_____
_____	_____	_____	_____	_____
_____	_____	_____	_____	_____
_____	_____	_____	_____	_____

List nature of duties/accomplishments in each assignment on the pages where information on each employment position is given.

Employment Statistics:

Immediate Salary Objective: $ _____

Immediate Position Objectives:

Carefully list in order of   1. _____
preference the titles of
five positions you believe   2. _____
you could fill at this stage
of your career. Then, check   3. _____
which two, regardless of
your order of preference,   4. _____
you believe you are best
qualified for.   5. _____

Long-range position objectives: _____

Past Employment: (start with first job)

	Company	Company	Company	Company
Name of Co.				
Type of Busi-ness/Products				
Division/ Dept.				
Approx. Sales Volume				
Location				
Titles Held				
Reported to (Titles)				
Dates				
First/Last Salary				
Reason for Leaving Co.				

Which of the words below best describe functions you perfomed in your last 4 positions? Double check (√√) those which describe functions you continuously performed, and single check (√) those which had application on an occasional basis. Please give careful thought to each word and do not exaggerate. Later on in this questionnaire, we request that you elaborate on accomplishments related to the words you have double checked.

	Present or Most Recent Position	Next Most Recent Position	Second Most Recent Position	Third Most Recent Position
planned				
directed				
controlled				—
established				
disapproved				—
scheduled				
systematized				
managed				—
guided				
conducted				
harmonized				
grouped				
wrote				
conceived				—
cataloged				
created				
trained				
reshaped				
supervised				
improved				
strengthened				
enlarged				
examined				
contracted				
straightened				
organized				
coordinated				
implemented				
approved				
designed				
invented				
arranged				
governed				
presided				
sorted				
analyzed				
distributed				
administered				
indexed				
developed				
presented				
recruited				
moderated				
expanded				
negotiated				
investigated				
rectified				
revised				

Complete This and the Adjacent Sheet
for Your Present Position

Company: _____ Position: _____ Dates From: _____

To: _____

General job responsibilities/
description. Be sure to in-
clude # of employees super-
vised directly and indirect-
ly, titles of individuals
reporting to you, also bud-
get, equipment and material
responsibilities, with an
indication of whether your
influence was direct or
indirect.

_____
_____
_____
_____
_____
_____
_____
_____
_____
_____
_____
_____
_____

Significant accomplishments.
Relate to sales/profits/cost
savings when possible (i.e.
elaborate on items such as
installed standard cost sys-
tem, guided development of
3 new products, developed
employee benefit program,
generated $50,000 in new
business, etc.) — expand
on the words you have
double checked (√ √) on
the previous page if possible.
(This section is particularly
vital to preparation of
your resume.)

_____
_____
_____
_____
_____
_____
_____
_____
_____
_____

*Describe any <u>original</u> reports,
papers, documents that you
prepared, or which were originated
under your direction:*

_____

_____

_____

_____

_____

_____

*List any direct or indirect
<u>technical contribution</u> which
you made or participated in:*

_____

_____

_____

_____

_____

_____

*List any of your <u>administrative</u>
<u>or procedural recommenda-</u>
<u>tions</u> which were imple-
mented:*

_____

_____

_____

_____

_____

_____

*List <u>major management</u>
<u>decisions</u> (not covered
so far) or <u>organizational</u>
<u>changes</u> in which you actively
participated:*

_____

_____

_____

_____

_____

_____

*Describe any <u>promotion</u> or
<u>transfer</u> to this position
with approximate date and
amount of salary increase:*

_____

_____

_____

_____

_____

_____

Complete This and the Adjacent Sheet
for Your Most Recent Previous Position Held

Company: _____ Position: _____ Dates From: _____

To: _____

General job responsibilities/
description. Be sure to include # of employees supervised directly and indirect-
ly, titles of individuals
reporting to you, also budget, equipment and material
responsibilities, with an
indication of whether your
influence was direct or
indirect.

_____

_____

_____

_____

_____

_____

_____

_____

_____

_____

_____

_____

_____

Significant accomplishments.
Relate to sales/profits/cost
savings when possible (i.e.
elaborate on items such as
installed standard cost system, guided development of
3 new products, developed
employee benefit program,
generated $50,000 in new
business, etc.) — expand
on the words you have
double checked (√ √) on
the previous page if possible.
(This section is particularly
vital to preparation of
your resume.)

_____

_____

_____

_____

_____

_____

_____

_____

_____

_____

_____

_____

Describe any <u>original</u> reports, papers, documents that you prepared, or which were originated under your direction:

_____
_____
_____
_____
_____
_____

List any direct or indirect <u>technical contribution</u> which you made or participated in:

_____
_____
_____
_____
_____

List any of your <u>administrative or procedural recommenda-tions</u> which were imple-mented:

_____
_____
_____
_____
_____

List <u>major management decisions</u> (not covered so far) or <u>organizational changes</u> in which you actively participated:

_____
_____
_____
_____
_____

Describe any <u>promotion</u> or <u>transfer</u> to this position with approximate date and amount of salary increase:

_____
_____
_____
_____
_____

Complete This and the Adjacent Sheet
for Your 2nd Most Recent Previous Position Held

Company: _____ Position: _____ Dates From: _____

                                                          To: _____

General job responsibilities/
description. Be sure to in-   _____
clude # of employees super-
vised directly and indirect-   _____
ly, titles of individuals
reporting to you, also bud-   _____
get, equipment and material
responsibilities, with an   _____
indication of whether your
influence was direct or   _____
indirect.
                                  _____

                                  _____

                                  _____

                                  _____

                                  _____

                                  _____

Significant accomplishments.   _____
Relate to sales/profits/cost
savings when possible (i.e.   _____
elaborate on items such as
installed standard cost sys-   _____
tem, guided development of
3 new products, developed   _____
employee benefit program,
generated $50,000 in new   _____
business, etc.) — expand
on the words you have   _____
double checked (√ √) on
the previous page if possible.   _____
(This section is particularly
vital to preparation of   _____
your resume.)
                                  _____

                                  _____

                                  _____

Describe any <u>original</u> reports,
papers, <u>documents</u> that you
prepared, or which were originated
under your direction:

_____

_____

_____

_____

_____

List any direct or indirect
<u>technical contribution</u> which
<u>you</u> made or participated in:

_____

_____

_____

_____

_____

List any of your <u>administrative</u>
<u>or procedural recommenda-</u>
<u>tions</u> which were imple-
mented:

_____

_____

_____

_____

_____

List <u>major management</u>
<u>decisions (not covered</u>
so far) or <u>organizational</u>
<u>changes</u> in which you actively
participated:

_____

_____

_____

_____

_____

Describe any <u>promotion</u> or
<u>transfer to this position</u>
with approximate date and
amount of salary increase:

_____

_____

_____

_____

_____

Complete This and the Adjacent Sheet
for Your 3rd Most Recent Previous Position Held

Company: _____ Position: _____ Dates From: _____

To: _____

*General job responsibilities/
description. Be sure to include # of employees supervised directly and indirect-
ly, titles of individuals
reporting to you, also budget, equipment and material
responsibilities, with an
indication of whether your
influence was direct or
indirect.*

_____

_____

_____

_____

_____

_____

_____

_____

_____

_____

*Significant accomplishments.
Relate to sales/profits/cost
savings when possible (i.e.
elaborate on items such as
installed standard cost system, guided development of
3 new products, developed
employee benefit program,
generated $50,000 in new
business, etc.) — expand
on the words you have
double checked (√ √) on
the previous page if possible.
(This section is particularly
vital to preparation of
your resume.)*

_____

_____

_____

_____

_____

_____

_____

_____

_____

Describe any <u>original</u> reports, papers, documents that you prepared, or which were originated under your direction:

_____

_____

_____

_____

_____

_____

List any direct or indirect <u>technical contribution</u> which you made or participated in:

_____

_____

_____

_____

List any of your <u>administrative or procedural recommenda-tions</u> which were imple-mented:

_____

_____

_____

_____

List <u>major management decisions</u> (not covered so far) or organizational changes in which you actively participated:

_____

_____

_____

_____

Describe any <u>promotion</u> or <u>transfer</u> to this position with approximate date and amount of salary increase:

_____

_____

_____

_____

_____

CHAPTER 23

Added Notes for Women in the Job Market

In recent years our firm has helped many women achieve unusual success. In fact, we have marketed women into almost all types of professional and managerial positions. These include jobs as design engineers, lawyers, production managers as well as stock brokers, art directors, general managers and company presidents.

Nevertheless, in the business world there still exists some genuine discrimination against women. Unfortunately, this is a problem which will only be resolved over a period of many years.

However, as an individual, you should not view your opportunity as being impacted in a significant way by this environment. Any woman seeking a new position needs to obtain just one job that is right for her.

Today, Federal and state laws, along with changing social attitudes, have produced immense pressures on large employers to recruit women for all types of responsibilities. Government agencies are requiring detailed reports which examine employer compliance.

For these reasons, the realities are that many companies actively solicit female talent, and in some cases they even prefer slightly less qualified females over male candidates. In a large number of firms promotions are also coming more swiftly for female managers.

Course Hazards

There are obstacles in the paths of women that men never experience. In the following pages I will briefly review some of the most common pitfalls: male chauvinism, sexual intimidation, and male condescension. Entire books could be written on each - and have been; but for this purpose, I want only to make you aware of the obstacles you might encounter and give you a few pointers to cope with them more effectively.

Male Chauvinism

In a sense, all of the obstacles encountered by women can be categorized as stemming from male chauvinism. Unfortunately, behind some people's biased treatment of women are beliefs that women do not belong in responsible professional positions.

Chauvinists tend to assign limited "female duties" to women for any number of reasons: ignorance, habit, limited exposure to different types of women, personal insecurity. If you encounter this philosophy, you must not allow yourself to show anger. It usually feeds the problem and "proves" to biased men that women are "too emotional" to fit into a business environment. Also, do not resort to defensiveness. The object is to prove through your efforts that you deserve the position.

It is a sad fact of life that some women still have to work harder than many men to get ahead. However, this is changing fast. If you feel that a company is irreversibly rigid where the promotion of women is concerned, then turn elsewhere. In the course of your search you will find many employers with a wealth of opportunities for women.

Sexual Intimidation

You should never allow sexual undertones to creep into any interview discussions. Obviously, some men may test the waters. However, if you laugh heartily at an off-color joke or accept an offer to have drinks at a romantic cocktail lounge, you will almost always jeopardize your chances for winning a good position. In fact, you'll generally do best by not acknowledging remarks which have sexual undertones. If you choose to respond, give a cool, polite response that signals your lack of interest in a personal relationship. Your ability to project professionalism will be the key.

In conjunction with this subject, realize that your over-all appearance is always an advertisement for you. If you are dressed in a professional and businesslike way, your interviewer will be inclined to take you seriously and interact with you professionally. If you are wearing provocative clothing, you're apt to create the wrong impression.

Male Condescension

Male condescension takes many forms. I will not enumerate them because you will recognize them easily enough. But what should you do if a man implies that you may be more appropriately suited to domestic responsibilities, or that you cannot be expected to understand what market share is all about? Frequently, such beliefs are expressed far more subtly. "Why would a pretty girl like you want to put herself in a business like ours?"

Again, keep your cool and don't respond emotionally. A factual response that chooses to circumvent this type of remark is usually most effective. For example, "I have discovered I have a great need for achievement in business. I think many women today get enjoyment from a diversified life that includes success outside the home." Even the first part of your response is sufficient if you wish to remain terse. Either way, you will have redirected the conversation onto a more businesslike path.

The most important thing to remember concerning chauvinism, sexual intimidation and male condescension is that you don't need to accept them. Make sure you read the signals and determine as best you can a realistic picture of the workplace. Today there are many good opportunities available for women, and you may be better off not working in that particular environment.

If you are still sufficiently interested in the company, you may need to ask yourself whether you are up to dealing with the problem. Will you be able to change a person's attitude toward you?

Some women become infuriated at the games played by such people and they overreact. That usually just aggravates the situation, and the likelihood of building a career in such an environment is slim. In short, know yourself first; then assess the environment and those likely to be around you.

Learning to Handle Subtle Questions

Even though the law states that certain questions may not be asked of a job candidate, they are sometimes asked nonetheless, and usually in a vague manner. As you probably know, our laws say that a job applicant may not be discriminated against because of age, sex, marital status, religion, race or national origin.

Still the information is sometimes gained through roundabout questions: "How old were you when you came to this country?" (after the candidate had stated earlier that she had moved to the U.S. from Mexico in 1949). "How long have you been known by your current name?" is a common way to determine if you are married. "Do you plan to have a family?" expresses the interviewer's concern over whether you will leave the job after the company has invested time in your training.

If a "trick question" is posed about your age, you can politely ask if the company is concerned about the age of its applicants. The interviewers will hastily assure you that they are not. Meanwhile, you have avoided answering the question.

Regarding your marital status, I suggest you answer openly to show the interviewer that you have read between the lines of the question and are very direct. You should use a subtle but dignified way to make your point.

In regard to your plan for a family, directness is once again a good prescription. Perhaps you haven't yet decided on a family. Then say so. Otherwise, state that you might well have a family at some future time, adding that it would be unlikely that it would interfere with your present career plans.

To be at your best in interviews, you also need to be critically aware of the reasons why employers frequently *reject* women candidates.

Aside from the fact that some men are threatened by women in business, the usual negatives include beliefs that women candidates are too fragile, not shrewd enough, short on ability for handling men, and overly emotional.

In the interview situation, women are also often criticized for talking too much, for making too much use of body language, for dwelling too much on family-related subjects, and for assorted personal appearance factors. Here I am referring to the obvious things to avoid; e.g. too much make-up, heavy perfume, tasteless jewelry, poorly manicured fingernails, trendy clothing, overly short skirts, and inappropriate hair coloring or styles.

I believe that any woman seeking a professional or managerial position should focus on projecting qualities of genuineness, intelligence, ability and drive.

Women should also strive to relate their comments to sales, profits and the other factors covered in the interview chapter of this book. If you can show an organization how to be more efficient or improve sales and profits, you won't be facing employment barriers very long!

Are Some Companies Better For Women than Others?

Much depends on your individual goals and personality, but I know from the experience of our clients that the answer is "yes." Obviously, there are product and service areas that will interest you more than others. But beyond that, companies do differ in their attitudes toward hiring and promoting women. Some key questions you might ask yourself are:

— Does this company offer courses or workshops which help women develop technical or managerial skills? Does the company offer *any* continuing education benefits?

— Does the company promote women from within? Have others been promoted to significant positions of responsibility?

— How many women officers are there in the company?

— Are there any women on the Board?

While I have devoted this brief section to women, I caution you against thinking of yourself as a segregated category. The more you think of yourself as a professional, in a career context, as well as a woman, the more confidence you will project.

You should also remember that employers are not encouraged by women who wear their femininity as a badge — or as a wound. They usually expect trouble from such people. However, they *are* encouraged by women who understand themselves, who have clear-cut goals, and who are willing to work hard to attain their goals within the business environment.

From our experience, women who encounter the most difficulty are those reentering the job market after a long absence. For those of you in this situation, the remainder of this chapter is intended to provide some basic but important insight.

Determining Your Commitment and Setting Longer-Term Goals

If you are just returning to the job market, the identification of sound career goals will be particularly important. This is especially true if your earlier work experience was limited. Also, if you are a "housewife," you may not have been previously oriented toward a professional business career. A shift in thinking about your whole life may be required. The tradition of working in your early years, having a family and staying home is undergoing rapid change. The pressures are both social and economic.

However, the concept of planning and managing a career is still a relatively new phenomenon among women and men. No matter what your objectives are, analysis at this early stage will spare you a lot of wasted effort during your subsequent job search.

One of your earlier decisions must deal with your assessment of the commitment you can bring to a career. To make this determination, I suggest that you ask yourself some of the following questions:

— Do I really want a career, or am I only interested in a job for a few years?

— Am I prepared to devote a great deal of physical and emotional energy to a career?

— What position do I wish to be holding 5 years from now? 10 years from now?

— Am I willing to maintain a light, medium or heavy travel schedule on the job?

— Am I risk-oriented or is security more important?

— Am I willing to sacrifice time with my family for my job?

— Would my family be supportive of my career goals?

— Can I solve the logistic problems of running a household if my job is very time-consuming?

— Can I make satisfactory child care arrangements for my children?

— Is mine a home where duties are shared by husband and wife? If not, will that affect my ability to devote a large part of my time to a position of responsibility?

The answers to these questions will help you to recognize the extent to which you will have to rearrange your priorities. To some degree, a review such as this measures motivation. It can also help you establish more realistic longer-term goals. Without recognizing what you're willing to put forth, you can't arrive at attainable goals. Many people fantasize about acquiring great responsibility and authority, but they could never make the overwhelming sacrifice in time, energy, and privacy that such goals demand.

If you have a family, it is essential that you discuss these questions with those who would be affected by the life changes that your new career will require. Not only will these changes impact those close to you, but such discussion can generate useful insights and raise new questions that should be answered. These discussions can also be a source for the reinforcement you need in order to take the necessary career action.

There are, of course, no right or wrong answers in such an analysis. For each woman the answers will be different and the levels of importance will vary. Also, as popular as the concept of a "career woman" has become, the life style is not appropriate or desirable for every woman.

Above all, each individual must decide what "having a career" really means for her. Some can enjoy a quietly successful career manufacturing and marketing scented candles out of their own home. Others would prefer to be a product sales manager for a large manufacturing company, traveling widely and working under pressure to meet quotas.

The initial bottom line has to do with getting to know yourself. How? Ask yourself a lot of questions and don't be reticent to speak openly with those who know you well. Then you can decide if you really want to begin building a career, or simply want to get a job.

Taking an Inventory of Assets and Skills

Once you've identified the commitment you are willing to make to a career, the next step is to take an inventory of your assets and skills. Too often women tend to underrate both their abilities and previous experience, because they do not understand how to establish a positive career path.

But if you do a careful analysis of your life's experiences, you will probably find that you have developed many skills through volunteer work, self-education, hobbies, part-time employment and even through running a home. Your first need is to precisely identify these experiences and skills. Once this is accomplished you can concern yourself with how they may be transferred to a particular field.

Don't waste your time by focusing on what you consider to be your liabilities. For example:

— "I only know how to type. I really haven't done anything else."

— "All I've ever done is teach 5th graders."

— "I only have a degree in home economics."

— "I haven't worked in 17 years."

Instead, concern yourself with the transferable skills that you may possess or the potential you have yet to fulfill. Unless you've lived like a hermit, you should be able to develop a long list — at least a dozen key assets that could be of value to potential employers.

Let me give you a few illustrations. For example, you may have developed organizational abilities as a part-time office manager and they might be valuable in production work for a local newspaper. Or, your work on a charity drive may have provided some experience which can be of value in public relations. Someone who is good at fund raising has probably developed the skills required to sell a wide variety of products or services. As a homemaker you also may have developed skills and success in organization, budgeting, communications, planning, scheduling, etc.

The key point to remember is that countless women have initially viewed themselves in a negative manner, but have managed to overcome these feelings and gone on to launch successful business careers. To do this they had to assess the degree of commitment they could make, then identify their own strengths and get a feeling for areas where these assets might be transferable. Lastly, they had to bolster their confidence and self-esteem, then set targeted goals and begin marketing themselves.

Of course, it is also possible that you must add to your skills if you have not worked in some years. Many colleges and universities offer adult education courses in specialized areas. You can study anything from accounting to sales, broadcasting to administration... and this can be accomplished on weekends or evenings, if necessary.

Setting Your Short-Term Job Search Goals

Your next step is to focus on short-term opportunities. To do this you want to learn everything possible about jobs within the field you have selected.

In the course of setting short-term goals, be sure to gather as much information as you can about your areas of interest. Talk to people in your primary field of interest; read about it and clip articles about people who have excelled in it. Find out which jobs they filled on their way to the top, and give some thought to trying to follow the same path.

As a general rule, I recommend you study all that you can. Books, magazine articles, television and radio presentations, university extension courses and seminars can help spark ideas for short-term goals. Take advantage of these resources. Don't be concerned if you change your mind a few times regarding your immediate goals.

As you consider alternatives in your broad field of interest, I suggest you telephone, write or meet with those who can provide the facts you need to determine opportunities available, skills required and salaries paid in your location. Don't limit your inquiries to friends and acquaintances. Seek input from several individuals whose success is recognized in the business community. One of these influential people may even take enough interest in your evolving career to become your mentor.

As your job search goals mature and can be clearly defined by types of positions and industries of interest, then use the system I have set forth in this book to run your campaign. In terms of the action phase of your job search, it is important that you review my comments on a few other areas which are worthy of your attention. These are covered below.

Learning to Build Contacts..."Networking"

Contacts made on the playing field, on the golf course and in boardrooms have been a great asset in the advancement of careers. While some men have ignored this avenue, others have put it to exceptionally good advantage.

Only in recent years have women in business found one another. Due to the Women's Movement, which encouraged networking, there is more pride when a woman hears of another's success. Use your connections and you will find that when it comes to careers, most women are eager to help another woman, often out of a sense of common cause.

Women's networks have sprung up in a more formal fashion as well. State organizations, college alumnae groups, professional associations and many others are expanding and can offer help to women in career matters.

Learning the Industry Language

Business talk is permeated with language that men begin to use at an early age. Some of it is derived from sports and tends to make a woman feel excluded. For example, "He's really a team player"..."He's just a rookie" ..."You can always depend on him...he never drops the ball."

As far as this language is concerned, don't worry about it. And don't use it if it doesn't come naturally to you. The language you should concentrate on will be the business terminology that is important in your occupational area.

For example, if you are entering the brokerage field, you need to know what "selling short" means, what a "bear market" is and which bond is called a "Ginny Mae." Every industry has essential terms, and you will not be considered a professional unless you integrate these words into your vocabulary.

You must also become conversant with terms in common usage throughout the business community. "Market share," "P&L" (Profit and Loss), "ROI" (Return on Investment), "Earnings per share," and "MBO" (Management by Objectives) are but a few examples. Reading the key business media (*The Wall Street Journal, Forbes, Fortune, Business Week,* etc.) can help you greatly in this regard.

Specialty publications such as *Working Woman, Savvy, The Executive Female Digest*, and the Association of University Women's *AAUW Journal*, will provide gradual indoctrination into this "business-speak." There are also trade journals that relate to a wide variety of industries such as banking *(American Banker)*, data processing *(Computer World)*, advertising *(Advertising Age)*.

Business publications can help you learn about both terms and trends. For a quick synopsis of timely business articles and book reviews, a publication entitled *Boardroom Reports* offers an excellent digest. Reading the publications cited above will provide a valuable information base and help you develop a general facility with business language.

Learning to be Assertive; Striking a Delicate Balance

Much has been written about the need for women to become more assertive in business. So much has been made of this that some women have attempted to become something they are not. These people have often ignored their personal sensitivities by becoming openly hostile. The fact is that most executives are "turned off" by overly aggressive people, whether they are men or women. Remember, being assertive has to do with making one's views clearly known. Being overly aggressive can easily be viewed as an obnoxious trait.

In the interviewing arena it is indeed difficult for newcomers to gauge the degree of assertiveness that will prove helpful in winning jobs. It should also be remembered that lack of assertiveness is a problem for many men as well. Still, assertiveness is more readily perceived as aggressiveness when it is exhibited by a woman. Tact and good judgment are the keys to finding the proper balance.

If you feel that you are not assertive enough, you may be well advised to read a few of the popular books on the subject, or to consider one of the many workshops that are offered throughout the country...but don't go overboard.

How do you determine if you are assertive enough? One obvious way is to list all the occurrences — both personal and professional — which left you with a sense of having been overpowered. Then describe the way in which you handled each situation. Finally, think of how you would have liked the incident to turn out for you and list alternate types of behavior which might have brought about the desired end.

A typical situation requiring tactful assertiveness is the one in which you must negotiate the right income. Some people begin meekly, speaking in a barely audible voice, not making eye contact and sounding defensive.

"I know your budget is tight right now, but I'm a very hard worker..." Immediately they have offered a counter-argument to their request. Worse yet, they probably fail to project competence, confidence or professionalism. A more assertive, politely phrased statement that reveals your interest, knowledge and potential loyalty to the business will usually be much more effective.

For example, you could let your prospective employer know that you believe in your potential worth to his business, and do so without being defensive or argumentative. "Having followed the company for some time, and understanding some of your administrative problems, I am confident that I could pare 25% off your leasing costs within six months. I also have other experience which I am certain will help me add to efficiency and increase profits."

In situations like this be sure to make it evident that you have done your homework. Also, that you are professional enough to keep the interests of the company in mind as you promote your ōwn.

As in so many other life situations, keeping the needs of the other person in mind is crucial. Take the instance when your prospective employer asks you how you feel about staying late to complete an assignment. Because you have small children at home who return from day care at 5:15 p.m., you know that it is virtually impossible to ever stay late. How do you respond to the question?

"Overtime? That's a real problem for me. I also feel that since I was hired for a 9 to 5 day...."

or

"Overtime? I know there will be times when I can't get a particular job done in the normal work day. Would you mind if I completed such projects at home and brought them in for review first thing the next morning?"

Your employer, whether a woman or man, will not likely be concerned with your child care problem. Your employer will be concerned with your sense of responsibility toward the job. He or she may probe to see if you can be counted on in a crisis, and in the interview may test the level of your commitment.

In the second example, by giving that type of response, you will have made your needs clear without becoming insensitive to the company. That is being assertive in the best sense of the word.

CHAPTER 24

Financial Planning Guide

On the next few pages we have put together a general financial planning guide for anyone who may ever find themselves suddenly unemployed. The original source for this guide came to us through the courtesy of the Dow Chemical Corporation and the T.R.W. Corporation.

We have divided this guide into three basic sections:

    I. Projected expenses during your unemployment.

    II. Your present cash position and your estimates of possible cash inflows.

    III. Identifying potential sources of additional cash through sale of assets.

I.   Anticipated Cash Outflow

Listed below are the types of expenses which are routinely incurred by most individuals. They are only intended as a very general guide. However, we have found that the people who work through this budgeting exercise are likely to bring areas for potential savings into focus.

One extra expense listed involves the cost of your job campaign. You may have to make allowances for typewriter rental, typing, stationery, stamps, extra weekly periodicals, phone calls, added transportation and extra dry cleaning. There can be little doubt that it will cost some money for you to find a good job. We advise that you budget the funds which will enable you to proceed with maximum speed.

MONTHS

Anticipated Outflow	1	2	3	4	5	6
Bills & debts outstanding	___	___	___	___	___	___
Interest on debts	___	___	___	___	___	___
Mortgage (or rent)	___	___	___	___	___	___
Life insurance premiums	___	___	___	___	___	___
Medical insurance premiums	___	___	___	___	___	___
Automotive insurance premiums	___	___	___	___	___	___
Other installment payments	___	___	___	___	___	___
Property taxes	___	___	___	___	___	___
Tuition payments	___	___	___	___	___	___
Club dues	___	___	___	___	___	___
Contributions	___	___	___	___	___	___
Gifts	___	___	___	___	___	___
Lessons: music, tennis, etc.	___	___	___	___	___	___
Food	___	___	___	___	___	___
Clothing	___	___	___	___	___	___
Housewares	___	___	___	___	___	___
Personal items (cosmetics, etc.)	___	___	___	___	___	___
Drugs and medical supplies	___	___	___	___	___	___
Household operations:						
Heating	___	___	___	___	___	___
Electricity	___	___	___	___	___	___
Water	___	___	___	___	___	___
Phone	___	___	___	___	___	___
Subscriptions/newspapers, etc.	___	___	___	___	___	___
Automotive expenses:						
Gas	___	___	___	___	___	___
Maintenance	___	___	___	___	___	___
Local transportation (taxi, bus)	___	___	___	___	___	___
Other travel	___	___	___	___	___	___
Laundry and dry cleaning	___	___	___	___	___	___
Entertainment	___	___	___	___	___	___
Barber/Beauty shop expenses	___	___	___	___	___	___
TOTAL — All of the above	___	___	___	___	___	___
Estimated job campaign costs	___	___	___	___	___	___
GRAND TOTAL — (anticipated cash outflow)	___	___	___	___	___	___

II. Present Cash Position and Anticipated Cash Inflow

Listed below are categories which help you assess your present cash position and anticipated cash inflow. Those items which exist as totals, rather than monthly income, should be evenly divided among the six months. Once you complete these estimates, you would proceed to compare your availability of cash with the forecasted expenses from Section I.

MONTHS

Cash and assets which can be converted to cash	1	2	3	4	5	6
Cash — Checking account						
Savings account						
Credit union, etc.						
Savings bonds						
Stocks						
Bonds						
Cash value of life insurance policy						
Leases (sale value)						
Land contracts						
TOTAL						

Anticipated Cash Inflow

MONTHS

Anticipated cash inflow	1	2	3	4	5	6
Severance Pay						
Unused vacation pay						
Retirement funds						
Pay in lieu of stock plan						
Unemployment compensation						
Interest from savings account						
Dividends from stocks						
Tax refund						
Collectable debts owed to you						
Income generated by spouse						
Income generated by children						
Income generated by part-time job						
TOTAL (Anticipated Cash Position)						

III. Supplemental Income From Sales of Assets

We mentioned before that you should approach financial planning with the point of view that you may be unemployed for some time. In completing Sections I and II you may very well find that you are not going to have the cash required for surviving this difficult period.

If your situation is very tight, you should obviously hold down many expenses which might otherwise be normal. Here we refer to things such as entertainment expenses, gifts, contributions, lessons for the children, extra telephones, etc. You could also consider a garage or rummage sale of unused assets. If the situation looks very negative, you may also have to sell valued assets. Listed below are some of the categories you might examine as sources for extra cash:

MONTHS

	1	2	3	4	5	6
Automobiles (second car)	___	___	___	___	___	___
Automobiles (first car)	___	___	___	___	___	___
Sporting equipment (boats, planes, snowmobiles, campers)	___	___	___	___	___	___
Expensive cameras (or other hobby equipment)	___	___	___	___	___	___
Jewelry	___	___	___	___	___	___
Musical equipment	___	___	___	___	___	___
Stamp/coin collection	___	___	___	___	___	___
Works of art	___	___	___	___	___	___
Unused furniture	___	___	___	___	___	___
Old clothing	___	___	___	___	___	___
Other equipment (unused lawn & farm equipment, appliances, etc.)	___	___	___	___	___	___
Secondary properties	___	___	___	___	___	___
Your home	___	___	___	___	___	___
TOTAL (Supplemental income)	___	___	___	___	___	___

Concluding Comments on Financial Planning

The purpose of this short guide is to help you identify those potential expenses which might be reduced. When you are unemployed, it can be difficult to channel funds to the places where they are most needed. If you may be unemployed for some time, it would be wise for you to consider early communication with any creditors you may have. If you speak to them before you get behind in any payments, you will probably receive better consideration from them as you go along.

Other things you may wish to consider include:

1. Borrowing against your life insurance policy rather than cashing it in. Most policies offer a lower interest rate than is currently available.

2. A single source loan to consolidate smaller debts. The longer you are unemployed, the more difficult it will be to get a loan from a financial institution.

3. If you are really feeling pressed, sooner or later you may have to consider selling your home. A respected realtor with whom you can frankly review your problem will prove invaluable.

At the time you find yourself unemployed, you should also check into the prevailing government programs. For example, the Federal Food Stamp Program, government programs for paying the travel and interviewing expenses of technical personnel, state funding programs and others.

CHAPTER 25

Reference Materials

Sources for Names

If you plan to execute a direct mail campaign, you will need to obtain the names of individuals and companies to contact. Fortunately, reference sources exist for virtually every field and geographical location, including many unusual occupations and places. I suggest that you first learn what publications are available that may be useful to your campaign, and secondly, determine how to obtain access to them quickly and at minimum cost.

The reference works listed below should enable you to identify the title and publisher of several sources you could use. Obtaining access to these reference works may require persistence. Your alternatives include the use of public and private libraries, reference centers within your company or through a business associate, and direct purchase from a publisher.

Reference sources for directory descriptions

1. The Directory of Directories
   Gale Research Co., Book Tower, Detroit, MI 48226
   (313) 961-2244
   (Describes 5,200 directories; updated every two years.)

2. Guide to American Directories
   B. Klein Publications, P.O. Box 8503, Coral Springs, FL 33065
   (305) 752-1708
   (Describes 6,000 directories in approximately 300 subject categories.)

3. The Standard Periodical Directory
   Oxbridge Communications, 183 Madison Ave., NY, NY 10016
   (212) 689-8524
   (Describes 68,000 periodicals & directories in U.S. & Canada.)

4. Ulrich's International Periodicals Directory

   R.R. Bowker, Inc., 1180 Ave. of the Americas, NY, NY 10028
   (212) 764-5100
   (Describes 61,000 periodicals and directories published
   throughout the world.

5. Trade Directories of the World

   Croner Publications, 211-03 Jamaica Ave., Queens
   Village, NY 11428
   (212) 464-0866 (also London U.K.)
   (Trade directories listed by continent, country and trade
   or profession. Also lists import/export directories.)

Libraries

In most major city library systems there are one or more branch libraries that specialize in business. These sources as well as the libraries of any undergraduate or graduate school of business, would be likely to have one or more of the directory reference works. Quite frequently, they will also possess a collection of the most widely used directories.

You should not be reticent about asking a librarian to order the directory reference volumes if they are not available. Libraries are a refuge for job hunters. Providing the materials that help people find jobs is one of the most useful social functions any library can perform. Most libraries will purchase any volume that is requested a number of times.

Many libraries will also have the *Directory of Special Libraries and Information Centers.* This reference work provides information about more than 13,000 special libraries operated by businesses, government agencies, educational institutions, trade associations and professional societies. Many of these are open to you. Your local library may be able to arrange permission for you to visit some that are normally closed to the public.

Stock brokerage offices frequently maintain a small reference library for their clients and prospective customers. *Standard & Poors* and other investment directories useful to job hunters are usually available.

Sources at Your Present Place of Employment

In large corporations, both the purchasing and market research departments are likely to possess individual directories. Mail room personnel often know which people within an organization subscribe to various trade publications. Trade association and trade show directories would probably be available from the persons in charge of those functions, and you should be able to borrow publications you need without disclosing your purpose.

Buying Your Own Directories

For your convenience I have provided a listing of several hundred of the leading directories which have been useful to job hunters. The first section consists of the state industrial directories, and those of Washington, D.C., Canada and Puerto Rico. Virtually all of these provide names and addresses of companies classified by product and geographic location, and include names of key personnel.

Chambers of Commerce and industrial development organizations frequently compile and publish lists of local companies. They will also know of firms that have new or expanded local facilities that need staffing. You should consider contacting the Chamber of Commerce in any community where you would like to find a job. The address can be found in the telephone directory or in the *Thomas' Register,* which contains a listing of all U.S. Chambers of Commerce. Following the section on industrial directories is a listing of general and specialized directories.

Purchasing your own copy of a directory is often a requirement if you are outside of the major metropolitan areas. Sometimes it is possible to split the cost with another job hunter you know. Buying a directory also enables you to be certain you have the latest edition. Old directories usually have an unacceptable proportion of incorrect listings.

Industrial directories

Sources of information include industrial directories, state Chamber of Commerce Departments, and the Chamber of Commerce of the U.S., 1615 H St., N.W., Washington, D.C. 20006.

Alabama Directory of Mining & Manufacturing: Alabama Development Office, c/o State Capital, Montgomery, AL 36130.

Alaska Petroleum & Industrial Directory: Alaska Petroleum Information Corp., 409 W. Northern Lights Blvd., Anchorage, AK 99503.

Directory of Arizona Manufacturers: Phoenix Metropolitan Chamber of Commerce, 34 W. Monroe, Suite 900, Phoenix, AZ 85003.

Arkansas Directory of Manufacturers: Arkansas Industrial Development Commission, P.O. Box 1784, Little Rock, AR 72203.

California Manufacturers Register: Times Mirror Press, 1115 S. Boyle, Los Angeles, CA 90023.

Directory of Colorado Manufacturers: Business Research Division, College of Business University of Colorado, Campus Box 420, Boulder, CO 80309.

Connecticut State Industrial Directory: State Industrial Directories Corp., 2 Penn Plaza, New York, NY 10001.

Delaware Directory of Commerce & Industry: Delaware State Chamber of Commerce, 1102 West Street, Wilmington, DE 19801.

Principal Employers, Metropolitan Washington, D.C.: Metropolitan Washington Board of Trade, 1129-20 Street, N.W. Washington, D.C. 20036.

Directory of Florida Industries:Florida Chamber of Commerce, 311 S. Calhoun Street, P.O. Box 5497, Tallahassee, FL 32301.

Georgia Manufacturing Directory: Georgia Department of Industry and Trade, 1400 N. Omni International, Atlanta, GA 30303.

Directory of Manufacturers State of Hawaii: Chamber of Commerce of Hawaii, Dillingham Bldg., 735 Bishop St., Honolulu, HI 96813.

Manufacturing Directory of Idaho: Center for Business Development & Research, University of Idaho, Moscow, ID 83843.

Illinois Manufacturers Directory: Manufacturers News, Inc., 3 E. Huron Street, Chicago, IL 60611.

Indiana Industrial Directory: Indiana State Chamber of Commerce, Board of Trade Building, Indianapolis, IN 46204.

Directory of Iowa Manufacturers: Iowa Development Commission, 250 Jewett Building, Des Moines, IA 50309.

Directory of Kansas Manufacturers & Products: The Kansas Department of Economic Development, 503 Kansas Ave., 6th Floor, Topeka, KS 66603.

Kentucky Directory of Manufacturers & Products: The Kansas Dept. of Commerce, Division of Research & Planning, Capital Plaza Office Tower, Frankfort, KY 40601.

Louisiana Directory of Manufacturers: Louisiana Department of Commerce, Box 44185, Baton Rouge, LA 70804.

Maine Marketing Directory: Maine Development Office, Executive Department, Augusta, ME 04333.

Directory of Maryland Manufacturers: Business Directories Office, Maryland Dept. of Economic & Community Development, 2525 Riva Road, Annapolis, MD 21401.

Directory of Massachusetts Manufactuers: George D. Hall Co., 20 Kilby St., Boston, MA 02109.

Directory of Michigan Manufacturers: Pick Publications, Inc., 8543 Puritan Ave., Detroit, MI 48238.

Minnesota Directory of Manufacturers: Minnesota Department of Economic Development, 480 Cedar St., St. Paul, MN 55101.

Mississippi Manufacturers Directory: Mississippi Research & Development Center, 3825 Ridgewood Road, Jackson, MS 39211.

Missouri Directory of Manufacturers & Mining: IDC Information Data Company, Watson Road, St. Louis, MO 63139.

Montana Directory of Manufacturers: Montana Department of Community Affairs, 1424 Ninth Avenue, Helena, MT 59601.

Directory of Nebraska Manufacturers: Dept. of Economic Development, P.O. Box 94666, Lincoln, NE 68509.

Made in New Hampshire: New Hampshire Dept. of Resources & Economic Development, Box 856, Concord, NH 03301.

New Jersey State Industrial Directory: New Jersey State Industrial Directories Corporation, 2 Penn Plaza, New York, NY 10001.

Directory of New Mexico Manufacturing & Mining: Bureau of Business & Economic Research, University of New Mexico, Albuquerque, NM 87131.

New York State Industrial Directory: New York State Industrial Directories Corp., 2 Penn Plaza, New York, NY 10001.

North Carolina Directory of Manufacturing Firms: Industrial Development Division, North Carolina Commerce Dept., 430 N. Salisbury Street, Raleigh, NC 27611.

Directory of North Dakota Manufacturers: Business & Industrial Development Dept., State of North Dakota, 513 E. Bismarck Ave., Bismarck, ND 58505.

Ohio Industrial Directory: Harris Publishing Company, 2057-2 Aurora Road, Twinsburg, OH 44087.

Oklahoma Manufacturers Directory: Oklahoma Industrial Development Dept., Manufacturers Directory, Rm. 507, Will Rogers Building, Oklahoma City, OK 73105.

Directory of Oregon Manufacturers: State of Oregon, Dept. of Economic Development, 155 Cottage St., Salem, OR 97310.

Pennsylvania State Industrial Directory: Pennsylvania State Industrial Directories Corp., 2 Penn Plaza, New York, NY 10001.

Puerto Rico Official Industrial Directory: Witcom Group, Inc., 210 Ponce de Leon, San Juan, PR 00901.

Rhode Island Directory of Manufacturers: Rhode Island Dept. of Economic Development, One Weybosset Hill, Providence, RI 02903.

Industrial Directory of South Carolina: State Industrial Directories Corporation, 2 Penn Plaza, New York, NY 10001.

South Dakota Manufacturers & Processors Directory: S. Dakota Industrial Development Dept., 620 S. Cliff, Sioux Fall, SD 57103.

Tennessee Directory of Manufacturers: Tennessee Dept. of Economic & Community Development, 1014 Andrew Jackson Building, Nashville, TN 37219.

Directory of Texas Manufacturers: Bureau of Business Research, University of Texas, Box 7457, Austin, TX 78712.

Directory of Utah Manufacturers: Utah Job Service, Utah Dept. of Employment Security, 174 Social Hall Ave., Salt Lake City, UT 84111.

Directory of Vermont Manufacturers: Vermont Agency of Development and Community Affairs, 109 State Street, Montpelier, VT 05602.

Virginia Industrial Directory: State Industrial Directories Corporation, 2 Penn Plaza, New York, NY 10001.

Washington Manufacturers Register: Times Mirror Press, 1115 S. Boyle, Los CA 90023.

West Virginia Manufacturing Directory: W. Virginia Office of Economic & Community Development, State Office Bldg., #6, Room B-512, 1900 Washington Street, East Charleston, WV 25305.

Classified Directory of Wisconsin Manufacturers: Wisconsin Manufacturers and Commerce, 111 E. Wisconsin Avenue, Milwaukee, WI 53202.

Wyoming Directory of Manufacturing & Mining: Wyoming Dept. of Economic Planning & Development, Barrett Building, Cheyenne, WY 82002.

General directories

American Men and Women of Science: Jaques Cattell Press, R.R. Bowker Company, 2216 S. Industrial Park Drive, Tempe, AZ 85282.

Business Capital Sources (1,500 sources of loans of capital for business and real estate uses): International Wealth Success, Inc., 24 Canterbury Road, Rockville Centre, NY 11570.

Central Atlantic States Manufacturers Directory (manufacturers by state & product with executive names): Seaboard Publishing Company, Inc., 714 E. Pratt Street, Baltimore, MD 21202.

Directory of New England Manufacturers (27,000 companies classified by state and industry with executive names): George D. Hall Company, 20 Kilby Street, Boston, MA 02109.

Dun & Bradstreet Million Dollar Directories (3 volumes: Vol. 1—firms with net worth over $1.2 million; Vol. 2—firms with net worth between $900 thousand to $1.2 million; Vol. 3—firms with net worth between $500—$900 thousand. Listings give locations, products, executive names, number of employees.) Dun & Bradstreet, 99 Church St., New York, NY 10017.

Guide to Venture Capital Sources (600 firms with key individuals to contact): Capital Publishing Corporation, 2 Laurel Ave., Wellesley Hills, MA 02181.

Standard & Poor's Register of Corporations Directors & Executives (260,500 key executives in 32,000 leading companies cross referenced by product and company location. Includes home addresses of executives plus title and duties): Standard & Poor's Corp., 345 Hudson St., New York, NY 10014.

Standard Directory of Advertisers: National Register Publishing Co., 5201 Old Orchard Road, Skokie, IL 60077.

Thomas' Register (100,000 manufacturers by product and location, all U.S. Chambers of Commerce): Thomas Publishing Co., 1 Penn Plaza, New York, NY 10001.

Who's Who in Finance & Industry: Marquis Who's Who Inc., 200 East Ohio Street, Chicago, IL 60611.

Specialized directories

Advertising

Standard Directory of Advertising Agencies (4,400 leading advertising agencies in U.S. with key executives, major accounts, geographic index): National Register Publishing Co., Inc., 5201 Old Orchard Rd., Skokie, IL 60077.

Who's Who in Advertising (10,000 alphabetically arranged biographical sketches): Redfield Publishing Company, Who's Who in Advertising, P.O. Box 1256, Brattleboro, VT 05301.

Aerospace

Aviation Week & Space Technology — Marketing Directory Issue (5,000 manufacturers and service firms concerned with aviation and space technology, with executives): McGraw—Hill, Inc., 1221 Avenue of the Americas, New York, NY 10020.

Apparel

American Apparel Manufacturer's Association Directory (800 clothing manufacturers; suppliers of goods & services to manufacturers): American Apparel Manufacturers Association, 1611 N. Kent Street, Arlington, VA 22209.

Automobile Industry

Ward's Who's Who Among U.S. Motor Vehicle Manufacturers (auto industry executives): Ward's Communications, Inc., 28 W. Adams St., Detroit, MI 48226.

Banking

American Bank Directory (14,800 banks with officers and directors): National Edition & Individual States Editions, McFadden Business Publications, 6364 Warren Drive, Norcross, GA 30093.

Banker's Almanac & Yearbook (international commercial banks with executives & directors): IPC America Inc., Room 1705, 205 East 42nd St., New York, New York, 10017.

Canada

Canadian Key Business Directory (17,000 companies with chief executive officer): Dun & Bradstreet Canada Limited/Limitee, Marketing Services Division, 415 Yonge St., Suite 1107, Toronto, Ontario, Canada M5B2E7.

Chemicals

Chemical Executive Directory (300 companies with executive names): Executive Directories, Box 234, Kenilworth, IL 60043.

Construction

A.G.C. Directory Issue (major contracting firms by state with key executives): Associated General Contractors of America, 1957 East Street, N.W., Washington , D.C. 20006.

Drugs

Pharmaceutical Marketers Directory (lists company names, addresses, phone numbers, ad agencies): Fisher-Stevens, Inc., 120 Brighton Rd., Clifton, NJ 07012.

Executive Directory of the U.S. Pharmaceutical Industry (650 companies, 6000 executives): Chemical Economic Service, Box 468 G, Princeton, NJ 08540.

EDP

National Directory of Computing and Consulting Services (260 firms supplying data processing products and services with name and title of contact): Independent Computer Consultants Association, Box 27412, St. Louis, MO 63141.

Education

Accredited Institutions of Post Secondary Education (lists colleges and universities with names of Presidents): The American Council on Education, 1 Dupont Circle, Suite 25, N.W., Washington, D.C. 20036.

Electronics

Who's Who in Electronics (7,500 manufacturers classified by location): Harris Publishing Co., 2057-2 Aurora Road, Twinsburg, OH 44087.

Energy

Energy Directory Update Service (3000 organizations active in energy field with personnel): Environment Information Center, Inc., 292 Madison Ave., New York, NY 10017.

Energy Systems Product News — Buyers Guide & Directory Issue (manufacturers, distributors, and suppliers of power generating equipment): Business Communications Inc., Subsidiary, Thomas Publishing Company, One Penn Plaza, New York, NY 10001.

Engineering — Teaching/Research

Directory of Engineering College Research & Graduate Study (lists 200 engineering colleges with names of department chairpersons & research directors): American Society for Engineering Education, Suite 400, 1 Dupont Circle, N.W., Washington, D.C. 20036.

Food

Progressive Grocer's Marketing Guidebook (lists supermarket chain stores and major food wholesalers in 79 major U.S. markets. Contains names of key executives): Progressive Grocer, 708 Third Ave., New York, NY 10017.

National Food Brokers Association Directory (member firms with executive names): National Food Brokers Association, 1916 M St., N.W., Washington, D.C. 20036.

Thomas Grocery Register (manufacturers & wholesalers of food by product type and state): Thomas Publishing Co., 1 Penn Plaza, New York, NY 10001.

Quick Frozen Foods Directory (manufacturers with executive names): Harcourt Brace Jovanovich, Inc., 1 E. First St., Duluth, MN 55802.

Franchising

Directory of Franchising Organizations: Pilot Books, 347 Fifth Ave., New York, NY 10016.

Gas Utilities

Browns Directory of U.S. & International Gas Companies (executives of American & Canadian Gas utilities): Energy Publications, Inc., Division, Harcourt Brace Jovanovich, 800 Davis Bldg., Dallas, TX 75221.

Directory of Gas Utility Companies (U.S. utility companies with key executives): Midwest Oil Register, Inc., P.O. Box 7248, Tulsa, OK 74105.

Glass

Glass Factory Directory: National Glass Budget, P.O. Box 7138, Pittsburgh, PA 15213.

Hotels

Hotel-Motel Directory/Facilities Guide of the Hotel Sales Management Association (5000 hotel/motel executives, facilities, accommodations): Hotel Sales Management Association, 333 N. Gladstone Ave., Margate, NJ 08402.

Imports

Directory of United States Importers (30,000 companies classified by location & type of product imported. Contains names of owners & key executives): The Journal of Commerce, 110 Wall St., New York, NY 10005.

Import/Export

American Register of Importers and Exporters (30,000 importers & exporters classified by product. Contains names of executives): American Register of Importers & Exporters Inc., 38 Park Row, New York, NY 10038.

International/International companies

Directory of American Firms Operating in Foreign Countries (4,200 American companies with overseas subsidiaries. Classified by product and country. Contains names of U.S. executives in charge): World Trade Academy Press Inc., 50 East 42nd Street, New York, NY 10017.

Labor Unions

Directory of National Unions & Employee Associations (lists unions with officers' names): Bureau of Labor Statistics, Labor Department, Fourth & G Streets, N.W., Washington, D.C. 20212.

Marketing

Handbook of Independent Marketing/Advertising Services (300 creative type consulting firms in marketing, advertising, packaging, media, and new products fields): Executive Communications, Inc., 400 East 54th Street, New York, NY 10022.

Oil

Directory of Oil Well Supply Companies (worldwide listing): Midwest Oil Register, Inc., P.O. Box 7248, Tulsa, OK 74105.

Worldwide Refining & Gas Processing Directory: Petroleum Publishing Co. Box 1260, Tulsa, OK 74101.

Paper

Paper Industry Management Association Directory of Members (pulp and paper mill executives): Paper Industry Management Association, 2400 E. Oakton St., Arlington Heights, IL 60005.

Public Relations

O'Dwyer's Directory of Public Relations Firms (900 public relations firms with principal executives and branch offices): J.R. O'Dwyer Company, Inc., 271 Madison Ave., New York, NY 10016.

Publishing

For directories in the publishing field write to R.R. Bowker Company, 1180 Avenue of the Americas, New York, NY 10036.

Recreation

Sporting Goods Dealer's Register (300 sporting goods wholesalers, 100 importers, 800 manufacturers' representatives): Sporting Goods Publishing Company, 1212 N. Lindbergh, St. Louis, MO 63166.

Research

Research Centers Directory (6300 research centers in all fields. Include names of research directors): Gale Research, Book Tower, Detroit, MI 48226.

Retailing

Fairchild's Financial Manual of Retail Stores (500 publicly held companies with corporate officers): Fairchild Books, Fairchild Publications, Inc., 7 E. 12th St., New York, NY 10003.

Textiles

Davison's Textile Directory (Textile Mills & Dyers with executives' names): Davison's Publishing Company, 175 Rock Road, Glen Rock, NJ 07452.

Transportation

Moody's Transportation Manual (1000 transportation companies with names of principal executives): Moody's Investors Service, Inc., 99 Church St., New York, NY 10007.

CHAPTER 26

Plan of Action/Summary and Forms

Scheduling a Plan of Action

It is impossible to prepare an exact lay-out of all the campaign steps which you may require. Every person's situation varies in terms of employment objectives, marketability and available alternatives. However, the schedule below is a plan of action which has provided useful guidance for job campaigns in most salary ranges.

Preliminary Items — recommended for completion before campaign starts

* Review your strengths and weaknesses; job likes and dislikes; and personal job satisfaction needs. Identify the full range of your career and industry options and formulate clear income, title and responsibility goals.

* Learn everything you can about job and career change techniques.

* Establish a step-by-step marketing action plan, complete with a time schedule, and allocate as much time as possible to its execution.

* Develop your data base. Scan or complete the questionnaire for resume development and also carefully review the resume examples.

* Choose a resume style and sketch lay-outs.

* Prepare copy draft for one or more resumes (depending on how many different objectives and audiences you may have).

* If necessary, have it set in type.

* Select paper and order letterhead, envelopes, blank stock and have your resume(s) printed.

* Develop key resume copy in letter form. Prepare as many standard letters as you need for your different goals.

* Also determine if you will need an additional anonymous resume or special material for agencies. If so, develop them from the same information that is in your basic resume.

* If you plan to conduct a campaign in secrecy, get a post office box number or make an arrangement with a third party.

* In addition, different standard letters may be required for:

   1. Sending direct to firms (with or without resume attached).

   2. Sending to executive search firms (ditto above).

   3. Sending to firms with serious problems (ditto above).

   4. Answering ads (to be used in lieu of your resume when the position available differs from your resume orientation).

* Develop short standard cover letters to accompany resumes as an alternative to the above.

* Prepare a list of the employer addresses and individuals you will contact which includes:

   1. Your very best prospects.

   2. Your next best prospects.

   3. Prime prospects (from allied industries, growth firms, etc.).

   4. Secondary prospects (unrelated or requiring relocation, etc.).

5. Executive search firms.

6. Firms with serious problems.

7. Recently promoted executives and their former employers.

8. Prominent alumni.

* Begin cultivating or renewing personal and business contacts which may be useful, and keep a record of them.

* Check your references (if necessary).

* Subscribe to newspapers which list employment opportunities. Also search out and identify media opportunities.

* Make arrangements for typing assistance throughout your campaign. Have all your initial mailing materials typed (use advance dating if necessary), signed, sealed and ready for distribution.

* Check in libraries for job ads appearing in the last 10 weeks (including advertisements for positions senior to your qualifications and also those which you may have previously answered with other materials).

* Scan books on psychological testing.

* Develop your SODAR and prepare answers for potentially difficult interviewing questions. Practice them out loud if you are not sure of yourself.

Initiation of Campaign

* Mail all materials which have been prepared. (Be sure letters are marked "Private and Confidential" if directed to corporate presidents.) Remember that it is best to concentrate efforts in a short period of time.

* Check current display and classified advertisements (under various headings) but delay a short period before answering.

* Attempt to identify blind advertisements and approach companies on a direct basis.

* Check with editors of both general and trade newsletters.

* Contact employment agencies in reference to specific listings.

* Follow-up important initial correspondence which either went unanswered or resulted in a rejection form letter.

* Approach personal and business contacts. Inform them of your plans and objectives.

* Consider dramatic approaches (use of phone, messenger, telegram, etc.).

* Consider advertisements concerning your own availability. Check the success of other advertisements in the media you are considering.

Concluding Comments

The two prime objectives of any job search must include the generation of both interviews and job offers. Before you attempt to do this, however, you will need to assess your marketability, identify your career industry options, and formulate your job search goals. At the same time you should gain a thorough knowledge of job and career change techniques. Your next step would be to map out the plan for your campaign. By having developed a step-by-step marketing action plan you will be able to free yourself from many of the frustrations which commonly plague job hunters.

During your job search itself, you will need to be a good record keeper. You should record all correspondence and maintain a diary of the names, phone numbers and dates of each contact you make. Some examples of forms to assist you are provided at the back of this book. Even if you get an excellent job, these names will be invaluable if you ever have to look for a position again.

If you choose to execute a direct contact campaign, you must resist the temptation to use form letters. The personal nature of individually typed materials will always more than compensate for the extra expense required.

When you go on interviews you should always be well prepared. You must also be physically and psychologically confident. You should radiate enthusiasm and speak and gesture with authority.

Also, never underestimate the importance of your appearance. You should always look like a winner. Despite everything else, there is nothing that can be more singularly decisive. If you happen to be tired, unshaven, or wearing an old suit, be sure to postpone any scheduled interviews. Also, beards, mustaches, and long sideburns must be well groomed.

If you are attempting to relocate in a distant country or state, you will have to work exceptionally hard. You may also have to use every possible channel for getting interviews and should plan on executing a large campaign. This will compensate for the smaller percentage of response which you will probably experience.

When you are in an isolated location, it is even more imperative that you do everything within a very concentrated time period. This will enable you to maximize the number of interviews which you can explore on a given trip.

If you're going to do a campaign, you should try to conduct it while you are employed. Once you are unemployed, job hunting will be much more difficult. Also, as a general rule, I do not think that employed people who execute a large campaign should accept the first offer.

However, if you find something attractive and you accept it, keep your resume circulating for a while. This is nothing but pure and simple insurance.

During your job campaign keep an exact record of all job search expenses. In the past, these expenses have only been tax deductible if you actually accepted and began new employment. However, recent tax decisions allow that job hunting expenses will be acceptable deductions in all situations other than extreme career changes.

For example, under Treasury regulation S1.162-1, expenses incurred by an individual in seeking new employment in a "continuing trade or business" are deductible for income tax purposes. (If you are presently unemployed, the trade or business you are seeking would technically need to consist of the general type of services you previously performed.) Normally, the job seeking travel and transportation expenses you incur would be deductions to adjusted gross income, while all of your other job seeking expenses would be treated as itemized deductions.

In addition, if you accept new employment which requires that you move an additional 50 miles, you can deduct all related moving expenses. In order to take advantage of this, you must stay in your new job for at least 9 months following your move. The moving expenses which can be deducted include all charges from the household goods shipper, along with all related travel and lodging expenses up to $2,500. When you file your income tax, you should attach form 3903 which covers moving expense adjustments.

This book has summarized methods which have helped tens of thousands of people to successfully change jobs and careers. What you need to do is take the ideas set forth and tailor them to your own situation. To do a job campaign right requires creativity, hard work and a lot of patience. However, if you value your career, the investment of both time and money that you make in yourself will help you make the most of the rest of your life.

My best wishes for success in your job search adventure.

Executive search firms to contact

Name & Address of Firm	Individual & Title	Contact Date	(✓) If Reply Rec'd	Follow-up (✓) & Date	Interviewed by Date & Phone #	Referred to: Person & Company

Employment agencies to contact

Name & Address of Firm	Individual & Title	Contact Date	(√) If Reply Rec'd	Interviewed by Date & Phone #	Referred to: Person & Company

Employers and individuals to contact

Name & Address of Employer	Individual & Title	Source for Name (i.e. Directory, Personal, etc.)	Contact Date	(✓) If Reply Rec'd	Follow-up (✓) & Date	Interviewed by Date & Phone

Advertisements answered

Name & Address of Firm or Box # of Blind Ad	Where Ad Appeared Publication & Date	Date Answered	(✓) If Reply Rec'd	Follow-up (✓) & Date	Interviewed by & Date

Additional information for corporations

Performance Dynamics International specializes in Corporate Outplacement Consulting. As such, the firm is retained exclusively by organizations who wish to provide outplacement marketing services to individuals leaving firms.

Executives who periodically deal with termination decisions, as well as individuals involved in human resources, are invited to call or write Mr. Ron Colvin, Executive Vice President, for information on the full range of our Outplacement Programs.

Additional information for individuals

Robert Jameson Associates is an affiliate of Performance Dynamics and is engaged in providing personal marketing assistance to individuals. Robert Jameson Associates also maintains a Senior Executive Division that specializes in the marketing of top management executives into new positions.

Individuals who would like to learn more about the marketing services of Robert Jameson Associates are invited to call or write Mr. Edward Bandtlow, President of RJA.

PerformanceDynamics International
Robert Jameson Associates

Corporate Headquarters
400 Lanidex Plaza, Parsippany, NJ 07054
Telephone: (201) 887-8800

Other offices in: Atlanta (404) 396-9292; Birmingham (205) 870-0290; Chicago (312) 693-0100; Cincinnati (513) 721-6660; Cleveland (216) 447-1126; Columbus (614) 888-5515; Dallas (214) 386-7755; Detroit (313) 352-5111; Ft. Lauderdale (305) 527-1133; Houston (713) 871-8555; Kansas City (913) 648-0057; Long Island (516) 249-1800; Louisville (502) 425-0011; Milwaukee (414) 784-8000; Minneapolis (612) 941-0050; New Orleans (504) 529-5001; New York (212) 686-7633; Philadelphia (215) 337-9677; Pittsburgh (412) 321-3400; St. Louis (314) 878-0777; San Antonio (512) 828-9661; Syracuse (315) 423-9666; Tampa (813) 872-0096; Washington, D.C. (202) 293-7606; Wellesley (617) 237-2350